CREATIVE

An index
of **150+**
concepts,
images and
exercises
to ignite
your design
ingenuity

SPARKS

CREATIVE SPARKS

JIM KRAUSE

HOW
DESIGN
BOOKS

CINCINNATI, OHIO
www.howdesign.com

About the Author

Jim Krause has worked as a designer in the Pacific Northwest since the 1980s. He has produced award-winning work for clients large and small, including Microsoft, McDonald's, Washington Apples, Bell Helicopter, Paccar/Kenworth, Northern Trust and Seattle Public Schools. He is also the author and designer of the Index series available from HOW Design Books; *Idea Index* (2000), *Layout Index* (2001) and *Color Index* (2002).

Other fine HOW Design Books are available from your local bookstore, online, or direct from the publisher. Visit our web site at www.howdesign.com for more resources for graphic designers.

07 06 05 04 03   5 4 3 2 1

Library of Congress Cataloging-in-Publication Data

Krause, Jim, 1962-
    Creative sparks / Jim Krause.
        p. cm.
    ISBN 1-58180-438-5
    1. Creative ability in technology. I. Title.

T49.5.K73 2003
600--dc21

2003049915

Edited by Amy Schell
Production coordinated by Sara Dumford
Interior and cover designed by Jim Krause

Amy C.
Andrew F.
Ash G.
Brian B.
Danielle M.
Evan K.
Jenni G.
Katherine B.
Paulette S.
Roberta K.

*Thank you for the
encouragement and assistance.*

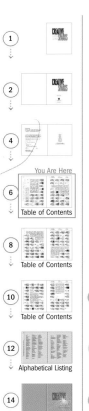
Creative Sparks is a resource book for people who equate the need to create art with the need to breathe and eat. **Creative Sparks** is an eyeful, a mind stretcher, an artistic fuel depot. **Creative Sparks** is not decaffeinated. Structured but non-linear; concise but non-specific; zealous but non-dogmatic; **Creative Sparks** is an artist's resource unlike any other and is meant to strike every viewer in a unique and useful way. **Creative Sparks** strives to inform and inspire without influencing the reader toward a specific method or result. There is a great deal of

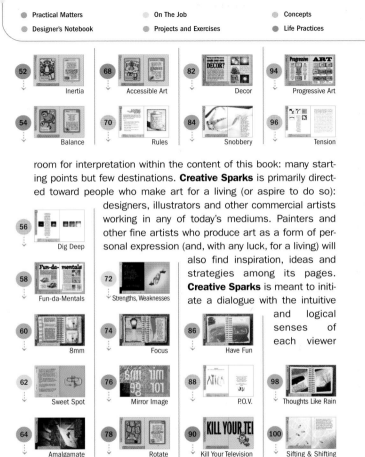

room for interpretation within the content of this book: many starting points but few destinations. **Creative Sparks** is primarily directed toward people who make art for a living (or aspire to do so): designers, illustrators and other commercial artists working in any of today's mediums. Painters and other fine artists who produce art as a form of personal expression (and, with any luck, for a living) will also find inspiration, ideas and strategies among its pages. **Creative Sparks** is meant to initiate a dialogue with the intuitive and logical senses of each viewer

Creative Sparks is a resource book for people who equate the need to create art with the need to breathe and eat. **Creative Sparks** is an eyeful, a mind stretcher, an artistic fuel depot. **Creative Sparks** is not decaffeinated. Structured but non-linear; concise but non-specific; zealous but non-dogmatic; **Creative Sparks** is an artist's resource unlike any other and is meant to strike every viewer in a unique and useful way. **Creative Sparks** strives to inform and inspire without influencing the reader toward a specific method or result. There is a great deal of room for

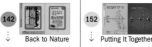

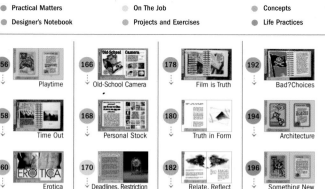

interpretation within the content of this book: many starting points but few destinations. **Creative Sparks** is primarily directed toward people who make art for a living (or aspire to do so): designers, illustrators and other commercial artists working in any of today's mediums. Painters and other fine artists who produce art as a form of personal expression (and, with any luck, for a living) will also find inspiration, ideas and strategies among its pages. **Creative Sparks** is meant to initiate a dialogue with the intuitive and logical senses of each viewer through a collection of both

(CONTINUED)

thing years in the business of art and design boiled down to a couple-dozen anecdotes, strategies and tips. **ON THE JOB.** From drawing board to board room, from laptop to desktop: practical strategies and methods designed to get the creative energy flowing expansively and efficiently. **PROJECTS AND EXERCISES.** A series of hands-on activities designed to take the reader back to the roots of his or her creative self and promote healthy artistic growth in a variety of useful directions.

CONCEPTS. An assortment of widely applicable abstract and concrete themes related to both the production and presentation of visual imagery. *Creative Sparks was both challenging and exciting to author. It is a book that I have been thinking about and wanting to put together for the past several years. I sincerely hope that it offers inspiration and motivation toward your own many and varied creative pursuits.*

Jim Krause

ALPHABETICAL LISTING OF TOPICS

CREATIVE
SPARKS

BEGIN WELL

You have already begun every project you will ever do. Look, listen, collect, learn, sketch, experiment, evaluate, bring in, throw out. Begin well.

FAIL-SAFE

drummer practicing LOUD & HARD.
everything can be heard from outside
the garage: every success and every
failure. drummer misses a phrase and
then repeats it in short bursts until
it works. i wonder: do the neighbors
mind listening to these sessions?
probably. does the drummer mind that
the neighbors listen (especially when
the drummer messes up?) NO! this drummer has ability and couldn't possibly
give a damn about what any listener

RELEVANT:

thinks about their drumming in the middle of a weekday practice session. if the drummer did care, they would never have gotten any good to begin with. as visual artists why should WE care so dearly about what people think about our art? what does it matter if we create something that sucks every once in a while? how much time have we already lost worrying about it?

PAYING ATTENTION

If the layouts and artwork we create are to connect with our intended audience, we must first try to understand that audience and then evaluate every aspect of our work in the context of NOW. What is "in?" What is "out?" To know this, we must become human satellite dishes: constantly tuned to the many (and changing) facets of style and form. We need to pay attention to what is going on today and what went on yesterday. Sources are everywhere: the colors being offered by clothing designers, the fonts chosen for a movie's credits or the pages of a well-designed magazine, the packaging of our music, the styling of our cars, motorcycles and bikes. Be receptive. Be tuned in to what's going on and notice who is responding to what.

CLOTHES
MOVIES
BOOKS
CARS
ARCHITECTURE
TEXTILES
YOU
FINE ART
MUSIC
HISTORY
PACKAGING
HIGH FASHION
FURNITURE

RELEVANT:

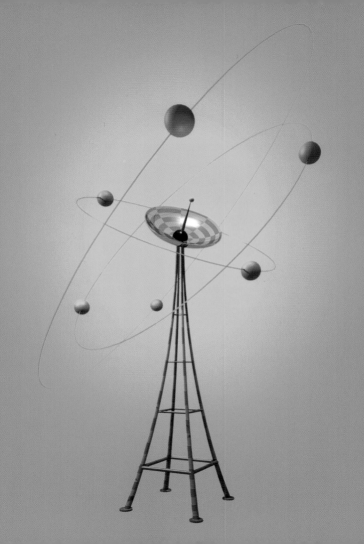

LOOSEN UP

L o o u p

WHAT YOU NEED:

The workday is all about control. *Bosses and clients telling artists and designers what to do and when to have it done. Control freaks freaking out freaked-out followers.* Maybe you'll have to do this exercise on your own time, but be sure to do it—you'll have fun, really. **Creating stuff that creates itself reminds us that art is fun and beauty can arise from unexpected sources.** When you're done, maybe you'll want to frame and hang it on the wall. Your friends might see it and think you're a genius. They might even buy it. Maybe you could sell enough of them to finance a permanent vacation from the corporate herd...

RELEVANT:

s ➡ e ➡ n

POUR

BLOW

DISPLAY

MAKE A PUDDLE OF INK. BLOW THE INK AROUND USING A STRAW. DO NOT INHALE THROUGH YOUR MOUTH DURING THIS STAGE. MAKE ART. CONSIDER LAYERING DIFFERENT COLORS OF INK AND USING DIFFERENT KINDS OF PAPER.

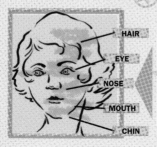

HAIR

EYE

NOSE

MOUTH

CHIN

Be sure to try this exercise both ways: with your brain and without

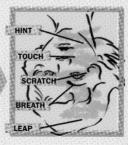

HINT

TOUCH

SCRATCH

BREATH

LEAP

CONCEPTS

CLENCH NOT

Avoid "clenching"
ideas that come to
mind—even if they seem
to be good solutions.

CLENCHED KNOT

Hold them lightly,
let them swim, squirm
and evolve. Good ideas
often morph into great
ones if they are given
room to play.

RELEVANT:

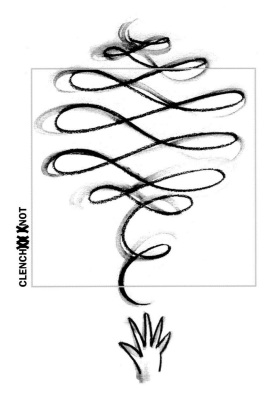

CLENCH 🕱 KNOT

NURTURE

RELEVANT:

Nurture Your Nature

01

Neglecting your **personal** time for art, apart from your **professional** pursuits, puts both your **personal** and **professional** creative growth in jeopardy.

Ask yourself: *Why did I become a designer, illustrator, photographer or artist in the first place? Wasn't it because you truly LOVE creating and seeing art?*

Tend your roots by cultivating the passions and interests that nourish your artistic core. Remember to take the time to pursue creative experiences and expressions outside of your job and/or career.

PERSONAL SHRINE

Personal

A SHRINE is a place or piece of furniture used to remind us of meaningful intangibles through the display of meaningful tangibles. *It's also a place or piece of furniture that can be an on-going art project in three or more dimensions.* How about creating such a shrine and spending a minute (or several) with it every day? Could a shrine improve your outlook on life (as well as your home decor)?

How about some incense and a candle or two to go with your items of inspiration?

RELEVANT:

Shrine

A shrine could be placed on a shelf, on the floor or in a cabinet. A used piece of furniture could be converted to hold meaningful books, beads, letters, candles, artwork, etc (left). A shrine could be simple or ornate and it should evolve over time and always remain fresh and relevant to YOU. As an artist, this is your chance to create a piece of meaning and beauty relevant to you and you alone. How often do you get to do THAT as a commercial designer?

A SHRINE DOESN'T NEED TO TAKE UP A LOT OF SPACE. HOW ABOUT PUTTING A FEW REMINDERS OF YOUR CREATIVE SELF AND THE VAST UNKNOWN IN A CUP OR TRAY? WHAT ABOUT A PORTABLE SHRINE? A KEY-CHAIN SHRINE?

When we evaluate any form of art or design, we usually judge it in the same way that we judge human qualities, both aesthetically and emotionally. For example, the proportions and curves found in an "elegant" typeface mimic qualities that are thought elegant and graceful (by society's standard) in the "ideal" human figure. A "crude" typeface often contains elements that bring damage and decay to mind. *If a trash-eating rodent could judge typefaces, would they rate their aesthetic qualities in the same way that we do?* People judge and react to advertisements and all kinds of visual media in much the same way as they judge and react to people. *Is the piece* honest? *Is it* condescending *or* pretentious? *Does it reflect* tastes *and* values *that are common with my own?* And, since all people and groups of people evaluate art in different ways, the commercial artist must take seriously the charge of identifying and relating to the intended audience every time a new piece is designed. Questions: Who is the audience for your piece? Are you a part of that audience? Do you understand their minds well enough to address them effectively? Are you using the right visual and conceptual "tone of voice" to reach them? What are they used to seeing and how is your piece the same as or different from what they have seen before? Are you talking over (or under) their heads?

PEOPLE POWER

A piece that features the right people in the right way can befriend viewers and make them receptive to the message being offered. Featuring the wrong people, or the right people in the wrong way, turns off viewers before they reach the message. Some strategies: Identify and feature the perfect person doing the perfect activity (perfectly).* Show a range of ages, genders and appearances by featuring several people in a group setting, by creating a collage or by using several individual photos. Consider age, race, gender, clothing, trend, disability. Avoid the overly-obvious stereotypes, insincerity and false emotion. Photography? Illustration? Stock or custom? Think about using an abstract style of presentation. Silhouettes or even stick figures. Consider featuring only body parts such as the the hand, eye or mouth.

*Good luck

RELEVANT:

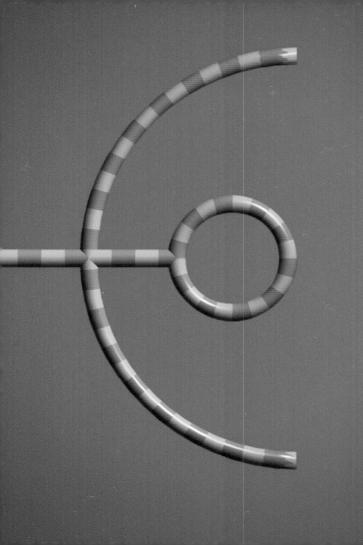

ARTIST AS VOYEUR

artists need to know something about humans if they are going to portray them and communicate with them. it can make people nervous, though, to be watched, observed. the man on the corner smokes a cigarette and watches the others passing by. people seem to equate smoking with doing something other than watching them; they pay him no attention. i don't smoke, but if i did i'd stand on the sidelines and watch people. maybe if i wore headphones i would appear to be "doing something" (other than watching you) and i could then have the same people-watching privileges as the smoker. worth a try. how about you--other ideas?

RELEVANT:

ALTER EGO

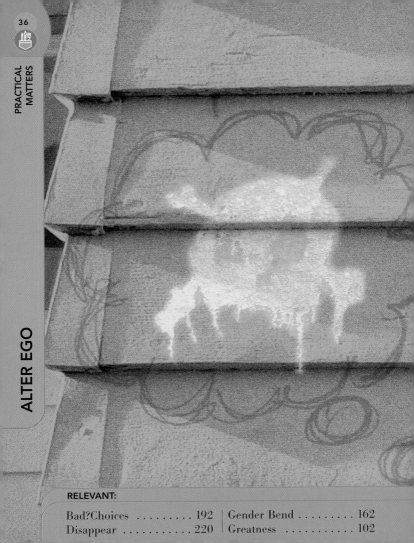

RELEVANT:

our art reflects who we are. But who are we anyway? What if you were to adopt an alter ego to fit the tone of certain projects? How about doing away with your usual pleasant self once in a while and creating from the dark side (or vice-versa)? Why not? Could this help you produce work more effectively given your current clientele and artistic goals? Actors, musicians and writers do it all the time in the name of art and so can you.

INVEST

Invest

02

RELEVANT:

Invest in Yourself

Think about it...how great a painter do you think you could become if you painted a still-life, even a simple one, six out of seven days per week for one year? How skilled an artist could you become if you spent that time drawing a self-portrait or creating abstract works of color? How far could your skills evolve if you made it a firm goal to shoot six dozen photographs per week? *Dare you imagine?*

What might happen if you committed yourself to a determined amount of time that was invested solely to furthering your artistic growth? Could you? Should you? When? Now?

FILLING THE VOID

The movie director begins with an empty screen. A composer brings sound out of silence. The sculptor sets their chisel upon a block of faceless granite and painters begin work with a blank canvas. All artists start from the same point: the point where nothing IS and something soon will BE. The difference between artists and their art lies in how they choose to fill the void, alter the state of things and rearrange raw matter. Everything matters: every element, every relationship between

RELEVANT:

elements, every placement, every stylistic choice, every color, every word. Everything we add to or take away from our artwork, both physical and conceptual, either builds upon or undermines our final achievement. Notice how the great artists and designers among us are the ones who are able to fathom and react to the endless depths of association that exist between all aspects and elements of their work.

BEGIN

As a designer, (BEGIN) a project by talking to the client and listening carefully to what they have to say. Take notes (clients love it when designers take notes). Uncover their assumptions about design. What do they consider "good"? What is "bad"? Why? Important: ask about the (target audience) for this project and what that audience is likely to respond to. If you have questions about any of their assessments, talk them through. Find out what your client's (competitors) are doing, how they are doing it and how well it is working. If you are meeting with a client on their turf, take a look at the surroundings. Does the office decor tell you anything about their tastes? After you meet, do your (homework). Visit relevant web sites and look through samples of (current and past) projects. Use this material to stock your mental (reservoir) with content ideas and to familiarize yourself with the visual and verbal lingo of the client's trade. Find out what you need to know about their corporate colors and graphics standards. Make sure (timelines) and (budgets) are understood. Make sure goals and expectations are clear. Let the client know exactly what you will be bringing to the next meeting and where you hope to go from there.

RELEVANT:

During a presentation, jittery clients are soothed by the relaxed confidence of a designer, art director or account executive who appears to have every aspect of the job under control.

CONCLUDE

Therefore, (CONCLUDE) the creative stage of a project by making sure that everything you will be presenting meets and exceeds the parameters and expectations that were set forth by the client. (Before) you present, try to evaluate all material through their eyes: better to identify and correct weaknesses before a presentation than to try explaining and defending them in the conference room. Within reason, (second-guess) every aspect of your design--concept, layout, execution, style, colors, typography. If you do not have the mental agility of a defense lawyer, establish a rationale for decisions that may be questioned before the meeting so that you can react with ease when the grilling begins. Make sure that corporate guidelines and production specs have been followed. (Proofread!) If time allows, let the layout rest for a day or two before you evaluate your work-- it's amazing what a (fresh) pair of eyes will tell you about your own work.

RELEVANT:

PACE

took a break from the art biz
for two years and made lattes
in Colorado. learned that a
good logo is easier to make
than a good latte. and logos
pay a whole lot more. my manag-
er was a 20-something woman
who rode a snowboard when she
wasn't minding the store. on a
snowboard she was really
smooth and really fast (a lot
faster than me and faster than
you, too, unless you are one
hell of a rider). at work,
though she never, ever seemed
to move quickly. she flowed
deliberately and easily
between tasks regardless of
their "urgency." the odd thing
was that she got more done
than anyone else, including me
(even though i was visibly bust-
ing ass all day). pace, ease,
focus, perspective. when i left
the coffee biz, i took that one
with me and have tried to practice it in the studio every day
since.

RELEVANT:

sometimes it's way faster
to go a little slower.

ICONIZATION

Iconization

THE SUN.
All earthly life depends on it. How many ways can you find to depict this Great Giver of Light and Life in two dimensions? How many Icons can you create to signify the meaning and beauty of this great celestial orb?

Build and broaden your artistic muscle by doing icon reps. Choose a subject and create 25 icons that depict its message and meaning. If that's too easy, try 50. 100? Sometimes the great ideas come right away. Most often, you have to sweat a little to get beyond the obvious answers and break through into new territory. Start with thumbnail sketches—drawn quickly on paper. Later (if desired) you can bring some or all of the ideas to completion using software. Be on the alert for still more ideas during the finalizing stages. *Tip: The next time you work on an icon for a client, fill a page or three with sketches before narrowing your search.* BEGIN WITH QUANTITY, FINISH WITH QUALITY.

RELEVANT:

FAMILIARIZE

Every time you design a logo, brochure, poster or advertisement, remember this: you are selling to an audience of experts. That's right, no matter how simple or complex the subject matter is, a large portion of the audience for that piece will know their product top to bottom, inside and out. *It's their thing.* When you begin a project, take the time to familiarize yourself with the product being presented. Learn about its history, its projected future, its successes and failures. Every product has its own clique of groupies: learn what they think is and is not cool. The web is a great resource for this kind of material and information. Ask the client for links and literature. This process will not only give you the background you need to communicate to the target audience, it can also provide you with a depth of visual and conceptual possibilities that you can access when it comes time to create.

RELEVANT:

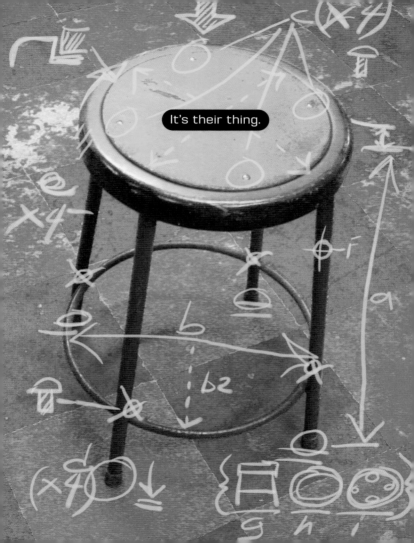

INERTIA

ART & REAL LIFE

03

Inertia

RELEVANT:

Inertia

Objects at rest tend to stay at rest. The same holds true for artists and designers. The most difficult stage of a project (especially a large or challenging one), is often the very first step—the moment when we simply have to stop making excuses and BEGIN.

There's no great trick to overcoming inertia. It helps to acknowledge what's going on in your head that's keeping you from working, but at some point you simply have to take the plunge.

Many an artist has found themselves miraculously breaking through to a higher level of their craft the day they mastered the Art of Beginning.

ART 3 REAL LIFE

BALANCE

Balance

Balance

04

Between opposites lies the path.

flexibility vs. structure
frenzy vs. lethargy
anarchy vs. order
insurgency vs. obedience
logic vs. instinct
simplicity vs. abundance
seriousness vs. silliness
work vs. play

The work we do as artists can be seen as that of finding points of balance between opposing forces and concepts and representing them visually. Sometimes the balance is confined to a narrow space, sometimes broad. Try this: identify the "extremes" that frame as many aspects of your project as you can identify and look for the appropriate points of balance between them.

Cultivate and value the skill of allowing thoughts and ideas to rise from your creative depths unhindered by the filters of logic, critique or worries about other people's opinions. Have you ever come up with a completely unexpected and fully useful solution to an artistic challenge in the middle of the night or just upon waking? How about while driving when your mind was not even trying to solve the problem? Where did those ideas come from and how did they make it to your conscience mind? What kept them from arriving sooner? What else is held in the depths of our brains?

Dig deep.

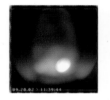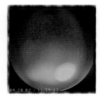

FUN-DA-MENTALS

Fun-da-

Painting helps you learn to see forms and colors. Learning to see makes you a more effective artist, whether you are a painter, graphic artist or a web designer. Still lifes are a convenient way to sharpen your skills with palette and brush. Look for objects of various shapes and textures and combine them into interesting arrangements. If you've never painted before, study a book on painting, take a class, or just paint.

It only takes a minute to set up a still life. That leaves plenty of time to PAINT.

mentals

Everywhere you look you will find subject matter for your next portrait: a chair in the kitchen or living room; the flowers outside the window; a vase of flowers; household utensils or tools; pocket change or purse contents; a sleeping friend or pet; a lamp, vase or ashtray; a coin or key; a lemon, lime or egg; a place-setting, with or without food; a car, bike or shoe; a crumpled piece of fabric or clothing. Take a look around, what else could YOU use?

DOING A STILL LIFE IS LIKE EATING YOUR CARROTS: IT'S GOOD FOR YOU AND IT HELPS YOU SEE BETTER.

danielle shoots her black-and-white short films with an old 8mm Canon. "you can't even tell if things are in focus until you get the film developed," she tells me. i think her films are beautiful. "it's NOT a

restriction." she says about her equipment, "when you work with low-tech, barely

functional equipment, you are forced to find solutions that are not the same as everyone else's; you HAVE to look for original ways of doing things. besides, i like working in 8mm. my ideas are 8mm size. i can wrap my head all the way around an 8mm idea. when i have cinema-sized ideas, i'll make a cinematic movie. i've been thinking though—i think i'm ready to try 16mm..." danielle holds a day job at a restaurant simply because the world is not ready for art this original and wonderful. she is a hero to me.

RELEVANT:

SWEET SPOT

The commercial artist must (continuously) evaluate everything they bring to the drawing pad or computer from the point-of-view of the intended audience.

It's as though there is a functioning "sweet spot"--a state-of-mind where a designer fluidly alternates between the role of performer and audience as they create.

Another supercharged midpoint lies between the logic-based mind that knows what a piece needs to do and the creative mind that brings its components into being.

Still another point of balance lies at the crossroads between the mental state of being too absorbed in your work and too far removed.

Pay attention to your states-of-mind when you work; try to recognize and cultivate the (sweet spots) that enhance the focus and clarity of your creative work.

RELEVANT:

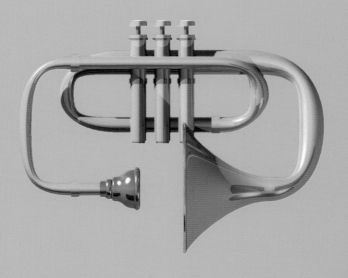

AMALGAMATE

3D

FINE ARTS

WRITING

MUSIC

POETRY

If you paint, what would happen if you incorporated words or type into your work? If you are a musician, how about adding visual media to your performance? What are you good at? What do you want to be good at? Think about combining your current and rising talents in new ways: **AMALGAMATE!**

MAKE A MASK

make a MASK

ALL YOU NEED: A ROLL OF PLASTER CLOTH*, WATER, SCISSORS, PETROLEUM JELLY, A TOWEL AND A FRIEND**

Here's an exercise that will not only get you away from the computer, it will also provide you with an exciting new piece of art for display.

**

*Available at craft stores.

One bonus of projects like this is that they remind us how to use our hands and our heads to create. You cannot press an "undo" command for errors. *But then again, are there "errors" when you're having fun?*

RELEVANT:

1. COVER YOUR FRIEND'S FACE WITH A THIN COAT OF PETROLE-UM JELLY TO KEEP THE MASK FROM STICKING TO THE SKIN. PREPARE THE PLASTER CLOTH PIECES BY CUTTING THEM INTO 1/2" STRIPS (SMALLER FOR FINER AREAS). YOU WILL SOAK THESE STRIPS IN WATER FOR A FEW MOMENTS AND THEN LET THEM SIT OUTSIDE OF THE WATER FOR A MINUTE OR TWO BEFORE APPLYING THEM.

2. START BY MAKING AN "X" ACROSS THE BRIDGE OF THE NOSE. REIN-FORCE THESE STRIPS WITH AT LEAST ONE MORE LAYER. AVOID GETTING WATER OR PASTE IN THE EYES OR HAIR OF YOUR PATIENT FRIEND.

3. GRADUALLY PIECE TOGETHER THE ENTIRE MASK USING STRIPS OF THE WETTED PLASTER CLOTH. BUILD UP TWO OR THREE LAYERS OF PLASTER CLOTH IN ALL AREAS. DON'T COVER YOUR FRIEND'S BREATHING HOLES.

4. WHEN YOU ARE FINISHED LAYERING THE PLASTER CLOTH PIECES, ALLOW THEM TO FIRM UP FOR A FEW MIN-UTES BEFORE CAREFULLY REMOVING THE MASK AND SETTING IT ASIDE TO FULLY HARDEN (OVERNIGHT).

5. DECORATION: THIS IS WHERE YOU CAN REALLY GO WILD. ADD "HAIR" BY ADHERING TWISTED STRANDS OF THE PLASTER CLOTH TO THE MASK. PAINT YOUR CREATION AND/OR COVER WITH METALLIC FOILS, CLOTH, GLITTER, BEADS, FOUND OBJECTS AND MORE.

ACCESSIBLE ART

ART & REAL LIFE

05

Access

RELEVANT:

ACCESSIBLE ART

Access encourages use. Make a practice of keeping art supplies within easy reach. Play by yourself, play with friends. Be silly, be serious.

What better centerpiece could there be for a dining room table than a container of colored pencils and a stack of paper?

Paper (in sheets or as a "tablecloth"), pencils, colored pencils, crayons, paintbrushes, watercolors, acrylics, water containers, glue sticks, scissors, old magazines, glitter, magnetic poetry, clay, rubber stamps, a digital camera or polaroid and film...

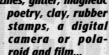

IN THE WORLD OF ART AND DESIGN, STRICT RULE-FOLLOWERS RARELY MAKE WAVES OR HISTORY.

Interestingly though, the best rule-breakers are often those who understand the rules best. It takes a clear understanding of the effects that occur when the "rules" of and design are broken to know when and how to bend or break them.

Suggestions:

> **Learn the rules of your craft from professionals, books, observation and practice. Strive to understand the reasoning behind the rules.**

> **Learn what effect(s) can be expected when those rules are broken.**

> **Follow rules when the result will enhance your meaning and message.**

> **Break rules when the result will enhance your meaning and message.**

RULES

RELEVANT:

CAUTION: CONTENTS ARE EXTREMELY FLAMMABLE. VAPORS MAY IGNITE EXPLOSIVELY OR CAUSE FLASH FIRE. DO NOT EXPOSE TO FLAME, SPARKS, STATIC DISCHARGE OR OTHER SOURCES OF IGNITION. ON THE OTHER HAND, IF YOU WANT TO CREATE A HUGE, KICK-ASS EXPLOSION, GO AHEAD AND EXPOSE CONTENTS TO SPARKS, STATIC DISCHARGE OR OTHER SOURCES OF IGNITION. HAVE A NICE DAY.

STRENGTHS AND WEAKNESSES

"When you train, train your (weaknesses). When racing, race with your (strengths)."

--axiom of competitive cycling

An irrelevant concept in a book for artists and designers? Hardly.

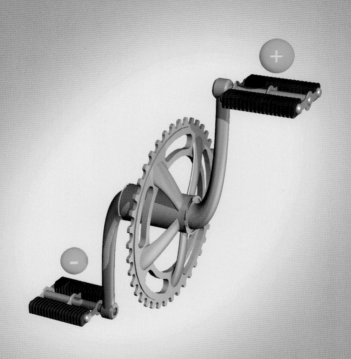

FOCUS

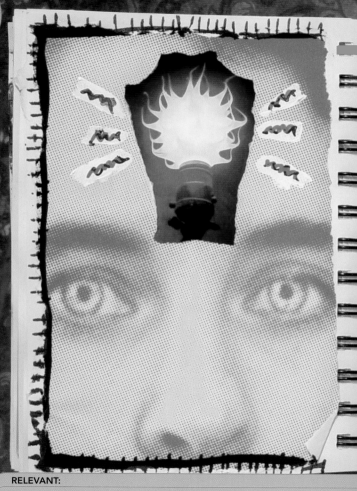

RELEVANT:

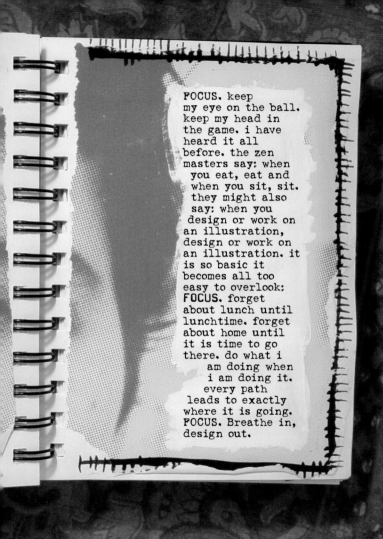

FOCUS. keep
my eye on the ball.
keep my head in
the game. i have
heard it all
before. the zen
masters say: when
you eat, eat and
when you sit, sit.
they might also
say: when you
design or work on
an illustration,
design or work on
an illustration. it
is so basic it
becomes all too
easy to overlook:
FOCUS. forget
about lunch until
lunchtime. forget
about home until
it is time to go
there. do what i
am doing when
i am doing it.
every path
leads to exactly
where it is going.
FOCUS. Breathe in,
design out.

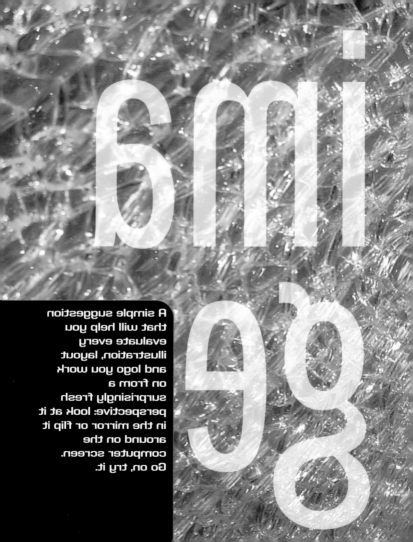

A simple suggestion that will help you evaluate every illustration, layout and logo you work on from a surprisingly fresh perspective: look at it in the mirror or flip it around on the computer screen. Go on, try it.

mirror

MIRROR IMAGE

ROTATE

RELEVANT:

Rotate Your Collection 06

Really, when was the last time you changed the artwork on your walls and shelves? Last month? Last year? Last decade? If you are like most people, it's probably time to rotate your collection.

Consider an easy-change system for juggling your artwork: clothespins, tacks, easels or metal clips.

Buy art from artists, galleries or second-hand stores; create art; display interesting objects; start an exchange program with friends. Try the cluttered approach. Try minimalism. Try glow-in-the-dark paint. Investigate self-hardening clays.

ENVIRONMENT

Does your environment influence your creative output? (Positively?) Could your working environment be improved without spending too much time or money?

It's worth considering.

Ideas: White walls. Colored walls. Walls covered with artwork, bulletin boards, chalkboards, posters, graffiti. Is it time to change the artwork on your walls and shelves? Windows. High ceilings. Happy lighting. Mood lighting. Lights that don't interfere with your monitor's display. Lights that are color-balanced. Comfortable chairs. Stools. Should your chair face a window, the center of the room, a wall? Should you stand? Chairs for visitors. A comfortable couch. A decent sound system. Plants. Water. Goldfish? Can you burn candles? Incense? Meaningful books: close-at-hand. BIG open tables, ready for projects. Fun art supplies, ready for use. Functional shelving. Photos from your life OUTSIDE of design. Funky collectibles.

When did you last change your screen-saver? Would you be better friends with your computer if it sported a hood ornament?

RELEVANT:

Why buy new stuff when you can
create your own
DECOR?

New furniture and furnishings are expensive and look just like everyone else's new stuff. Modifying used and existing furniture is eco-friendly and an excellent outlet for pent-up creative desires. Keep a cabinet stocked with glues, spray paints, acrylics, beads, found objects and other handy decorating accessories. Make your environment a place that honors creativity and inspires you to be *more* creative *more* often.

RELEVANT:

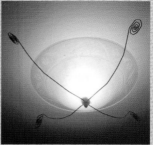

Idea fuel (counterclockwise from top-right): a bent coat hanger provides ornamentation for a simple light fixture · a ceiling fan with painted blades, screen-door-mesh light shades and beaded pull chains · a dart board made more lively with glued-on toy pieces · a rake head as a cheap and useful utensil holder · an ordinary light fixture made extra-ordinary with a gimmick light bulb.

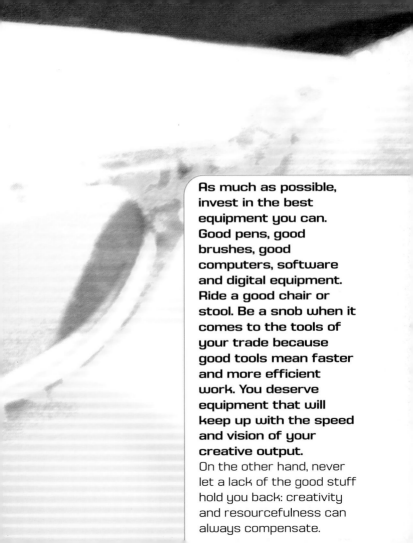

As much as possible, invest in the best equipment you can. Good pens, good brushes, good computers, software and digital equipment. Ride a good chair or stool. Be a snob when it comes to the tools of your trade because good tools mean faster and more efficient work. You deserve equipment that will keep up with the speed and vision of your creative output.

On the other hand, never let a lack of the good stuff hold you back: creativity and resourcefulness can always compensate.

HAVE FUN

CONCEPTS

QUESTION:
WHICH ITEM DOES NOT BELONG AND WHY?

P.O.V.

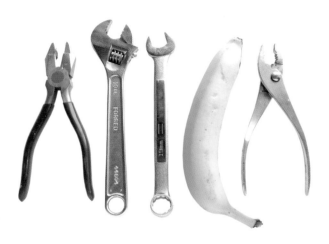

ANSWER:
The wrench: it is the only item that
cannot be opened.

The point here is simply this:
We are supposed to be artists and
artists are supposed to think
differently, right? Use your artistic
license: look for and consider
alternative points of view in all things.

KILL YOUR TELEVISION

KILL Y

KILL YOUR TELEVISION

LEVISIO

RELEVANT:

**N**It's worth considering, anyway. Not that all TV is bad, but life is short and there may be better ways to spend it than as a spectator.

And if killing your television is too drastic, consider neutering it—just disable its ability for reception and use it as a player for good movies.

Are you addicted? Can you say no to TV? Try it for a day, a week-end, a week. Give your TV a month's break and spend that time reading, creating, exercising, relaxing, dancing, meditating, socializing. After a month, decide how important television really is in YOUR big picture.

PROGRESSIVE ART

Progressive

TIP: BE SURE TO TRY THIS EXERCISE. Here is an exercise that teaches the artist to react rather than plan. To rely on instinct rather than knowledge. Transform and sharpen your creative instinct by repeating this exercise whenever you have a pen, pencil or paintbrush and a few spare minutes.

The goal here is not to create a thing of beauty, but to simply create. If the results are beautiful, fine. If not, that's **OKAY.**

A BOTTLE OF INDIA INK, A TUBE OF WHITE ACRYLIC PAINT AND A BRUSH (IN THIS CASE, A TOOTH-BRUSH) ARE USED FOR THIS DEMON-STRATION. YOUR TOOLS MAY VARY.

HOW IT WORKS. Begin with a blank piece of paper. Make a mark using the media of your choice. The next mark you make will be a reaction to the first mark. What kind of reaction? THAT is up to you.

AND SO ON. And so on, and so on, until you decide that the exercise is finished. **THAT'S ALL THERE IS TO IT. NOW DO IT.**

RELEVANT:

ART

Follow along as we go from nothing to something in 8 steps.

A big X. As good a way to start as any.

Circles, variously placed, contrast with the straight lines.

Thin, active lines provide action.

Dark areas for filling the void.

More fillers in an effort to find balance.

A few additional touches of black before bringing in the white acrylic.

White paint is added with the goal of giving the painting a lighter feel.

FINISHED.
Is it art?
Does it matter?

CONCEPTS

A

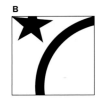

B

C

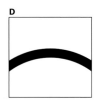

D

A listener does not have to be a musician to notice that something is wrong if an instrument is playing out of tune. Neither does a viewer have to be an artist to feel a sense of dis-comfort when certain rules of eye-friendly

E

TENSION

design are broken. Here are five examples of things that are best avoided if an eye-pleasing outcome is your goal. Note: this is also a presentation of five things to consider doing if you want to put viewers on edge. **A)** Elements that barely touch tease the viewer. The eye tends to keep checking the items to see if they really touch or not. **B)** The viewer's eye is lead out of a piece by elements that touch the outer corners. Also, tentative decisions create tension: the star is not quite level, but not very tilted and the small sliver of white space above the star's leg feels unsure, as if the designer could not decide if there should be a gap or not. **C)** Complementary colors of the same value (lightness vs. darkness) tend to "vibrate." Notice the visual buzz that occurs along the shared edge of the two colors as they vie for dominance. **D)** A horizon that is visually centered feels boring, static. A lower or higher placement would accentuate either the lower or upper portion of the composition. Note however, that sometimes an artist will intentionally center elements to create an intentionally static layout. **E)** By default, most viewers' eyes are drawn to the center of a defined area. That doesn't mean that the focal point of a layout needs to be at the center, but it does mean that the center of a piece is rarely the ideal place for empty, trapped space.

THOUGHTS LIKE RAIN

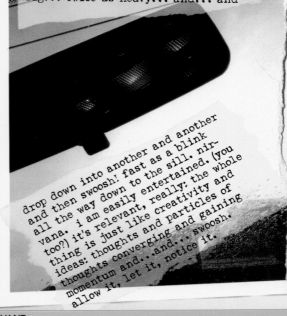

the car and the radio off. waiting and watching rain collect on the windshield. mesmerizing and so melancholy! watching for the next droplet that will drop—that is, the next one that will gain enough volume and weight to blob down into the one below and become twice as big... twice as heavy... and... and

drop down into another and another and then swoosh! fast as a blink all the way down to the sill. nirvana. i am easily entertained. (you too?) it's relevant, really: the whole thing is just like creativity and ideas: thoughts and particles of thoughts converging and gaining momentum and...and... swoosh. allow it, let it, notice it.

RELEVANT:

SIFTING AND SHIFTING

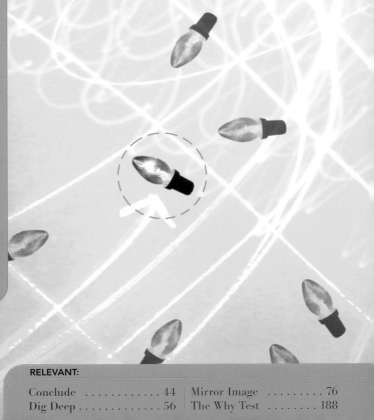

Encourage your mind to continuously sift through alternate ideas as you work. Mentally play around with colors, emphasis, typefaces and all of the other elements that comprise the piece in front of you. This can be happening in the background while your fingers handle the pencil, brush, mouse or keyboard. Don't stop sifting and shifting until the clock runs out or until you have reached the point where everything gels and points spectacularly toward the message being presented.

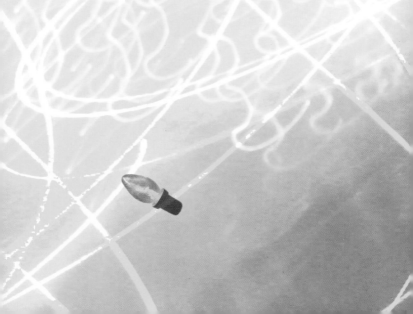

GREATNESS

The next time you are struggling with a design or piece of artwork, try asking yourself,

"How would this look if it were done by a great designer?"

Visualize it. Create it. After all, someone has to produce the good stuff.

Go ahead, take the crown out of the box. BE the King or Queen of Great Design.

RELEVANT:

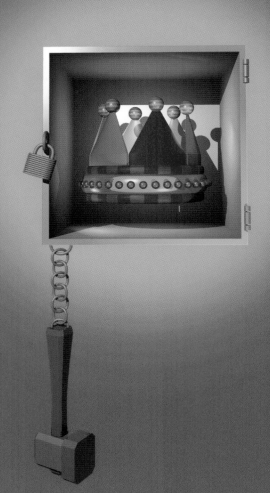

Font Love

A well-designed font is a labor of love and its curves, lines and serifs (right) are incarnations of aesthetics that have risen to the peak of visual evolution. To understand the thinking behind the construction of a single typeface such as Caslon (designed by William Caslon) or Futura (Paul Renner) is to understand the language of form, curve, proportion and visual innuendo. Don't be afraid of the "font geek" label, earn it and wear it with pride.

Many designers are surprised to learn that the study of typography is full of thrilling and exciting discoveries. Once immersed, they are never able to look at movie credits dispassionately again.

RELEVANT:

THIS MONTH:
Frame and display the letterform of your choice. Place it where it can be contemplated often and leisurely.

At right, a lower-case "g" from the Caslon Family.

NEXT MONTH:
Choose a new letter-form, contemplate it.

AMPERSANDS ARE OFTEN THE PLAYFUL COUSIN TO THEIR LARGER TYPEFACE FAMILIES. FONTS, CLOCKWISE FROM UPPER LEFT: GOUDY, BUZZER THREE, COLONNA, HERCULANUM, COCHIN ITALIC, COPPERPLATE, EX-PONTO, FRANKLIN GOTHIC, BERKELEY OLD STYLE, HOLLYWEIRD, HOUSE GOTHIC, GOUDY ITALIC, AND ZAPFINO (CENTER).

AUTHENTICITY

We no longer acknowledge an "ordered universe." Why should our art? To make such a demand nowadays is worse than impertinence, it is a travesty upon the historical being of the artist.

In the end the only authentic art is that which has about it the power of inevitability.

WILLIAM BARRETT, *IRRATIONAL MAN*

CATCH

RELEVANT:

We live in an ethereal ocean of ideas. Floating all around us, just beyond our physical senses, is every artistic expression that ever was, ever will be.

We never know, from moment to moment, when an inspiration or idea will hook itself on a branch or tentacle of our imaginative mind. It may not stay there for long before being carried off by the currents of everyday life, so we must be prepared to catch its message at a moment's notice. Carry a net (of sorts) at all times: a writing instrument and a notepad. When the muse speaks, will you be prepared to record its words?

For the commercial artist, the ability to
gracefully withstand the heat of
criticism is no less important than the
artistic skill they bring to a project.

When an artist appears unwilling to
consider suggestions from peers and
clients, they run the risk of being
perceived as defiant, lofty. Artists of
the finer arts may be allowed such a
persona, but commercial artists, because
they operate within a system where final
decisions lie in the hands of art
directors and clients, cannot be both
difficult to work with and successful.

Learn to hold the ego in a state of
suspension when your work is being
reviewed. Remember: a critic doesn't need
to know as much as you do about design in
order to spot a weakness or mistake.

Yes, sometimes you must take a stand in
the name of aesthetics and artistic
integrity: only you can decide which
battles are worth fighting. If you must
fight, fight fairly, respect your
opponent and know when to retreat in the
name of job security.

HEAT

RELEVANT:

ALWAYS AMAZED

08

ART SPEAK LIFE

Amazed

RELEVANT:

Always Amazed

Do you know people that seem to find something amazing about almost everything that catches their attention? The **artist** who possesses this quality is like a supermagnet for the nuts, bolts and girders that form the infrastructure of their creative work.

Become a curiosity junkie.

Amazement can be learned, cultivated. Amazement leads to learning and discovery. Learning and discovery fill your mind with fuel for creativity, make you a better artist and a more interesting person to invite to a cocktail party. Being amazed takes little time and little effort.

ART 2 REAL LIFE

THE PROFESSIONAL

Paulette (seen here with her son, Morgan) is the real thing: a designer who can design AND run a business. since i met her about 15 years ago, she has risen through the ranks of some of the

RELEVANT:

most reputable agencies in the U.S. and is now operating on her own for a list of clients that would be the envy of studios and freelancers everywhere. her work is outstanding and she has the awards (as well as the respect of her clients and peers) to show for it. **some observations:** college degrees in engineering and visual communication give Paulette a broad view of the world and an understanding of the way her non-artistic clients might see things. thoroughness and artistic integrity give her the confidence, capability (and when needed, flexibility) to calmly and effectively present her work to clients of all kinds. Paulette does not miss deadlines, does not do shoddy work when time is tight, and is willing to put in extra hours when needed. she has spent a lot of time looking at the work of others and exploring the bigger world. art is in her blood. (as a child, her parents would put a limit on the amount of time she was allowed to spend doodling.) rounding-out her visual talents, Paulette has cultivated a considerable amount of talent as a pianist. her favorite thing about running her own business from home for the past three years: **"being able to work in my pj's and being allowed to take a project from beginning to end all by myself."** who do YOU admire in the art world? what is their story?

Group brainstorming (two or more people) is a good way of getting ideas flowing and congealing into greater ideas,

but

group dynamics are tricky. Sometimes creative minds become overwhelmed by the flurry of energies that arise in a group setting and ideas can easily be lost in the melee.

A suggestion:

precede group brainstorming sessions with solo time. Give each member a chance to sketch or outline thoughts independently and in whatever way they wish. These solo sessions often produce radically opposed approaches and points-of-view. Then, when the group re-assembles, every participant is given a chance to share their findings and thoughts. Sometimes a single "winner" is clearly apparent, sometimes the solution is a combination of several ideas. To avoid conflict, decide how final decisions are going to be reached before you begin evaluating ideas.

RELEVANT:

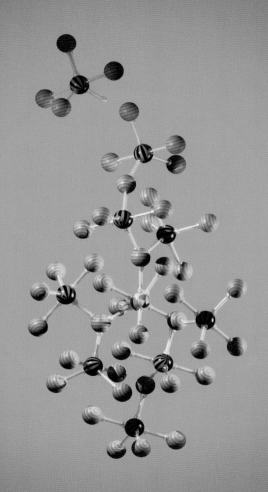

BRAINSTORM

Brainstorming is what you do before you start creating anything final. It is the process of tuning in to the wavelength of both the muses and the critics in search of possibilities, directions and solutions. You've heard it before and it's true: *there are no bad ideas when brainstorming.* Have you been giving this crucial step in the creative process its due? Are you accepting solutions that are too easy or too convenient before the search for something GREAT has been exhausted? Go for quantity! Variation! Risk! Adventure! Brainstorm with abandon.

RELEVANT:

Johannes Brahms often searched for musical inspiration in a meditative state somewhere between sleep and wakefulness. An assistant would transcribe his uttered verbal notations.

write.
write.
write.

Let it pour. The mind of a visual artist is often a busy and cluttered place. Offload some of the debris by putting pen to paper or fingers to keyboard. **Try this simple exercise: Write.** And keep writing until you've filled two or three (or more) pages. Don't let the pen stop moving for more than a moment at a time. Don't worry about what you are going to write, how it will sound or whether it is punctuated properly. Just write, write, write and see what happens.

RELEVANT:

now.

(If you prefer)

(maybe but probably not)

(always)

CONFIDENTIALITY

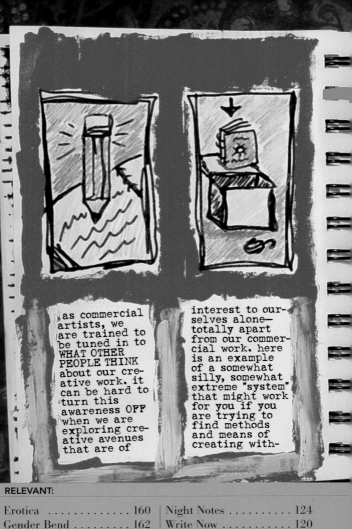

as commercial artists, we are trained to be tuned in to WHAT OTHER PEOPLE THINK about our creative work. it can be hard to turn this awareness OFF when we are exploring creative avenues that are of

interest to ourselves alone—totally apart from our commercial work. here is an example of a somewhat silly, somewhat extreme "system" that might work for you if you are trying to find methods and means of creating with-

RELEVANT:

out any sense
of self con-
sciousness:
write, sketch,
whatever in
your TOP-
SECRET note-
book. when it's
full, put it
in a safe-keep-
ing box with
all of your
other TOP
SECRET note-
books and add

a combo lock to
the box. now, in
the event of your
untimely demise,
pre-arrange for
a friend to drop
the mysterious
little metal box
in a garbage can
on your behalf.
simple as that:
no audience (ever)
and no self-
consciousness
now.

NIGHT NOTES

Night Notes

09

Here's a practice that you may or may not be familiar with:

Keep a notepad and pen near your pillow or on your bedstand.

Ideas that may have been trapped during the day sometimes percolate to the surface of a sleepy mind; creative breakthroughs can occur in the wee hours of the night; certain dreams and thoughts beg to be written about before they fade from memory. If needed, keep a small light handy, or simply write in the dark (sloppy writing can always be deciphered and re-written in the morning).

**Perfect
Imperfection.**

PERFECT IMPERFECTION

Improvement makes straight roads

But the crooked roads without improvement

Are roads of genius

WILLIAM BLAKE

CREATIVE SPARKS

DSC01271.jpg

DSC01272.jpg

DSC01270.jpg

DSC01276.jpg

DSC01278.jpg

DSC01274.jpg

DSC01280.jpg

DSC01281.jpg

DSC01279.jpg

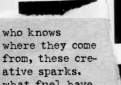

who knows
where they come
from, these cre-
ative sparks.
what fuel have
we stored for
their igniting
pleasure when
they strike?

DSC01291.jpg

DSC01282.jpg

RELEVANT:

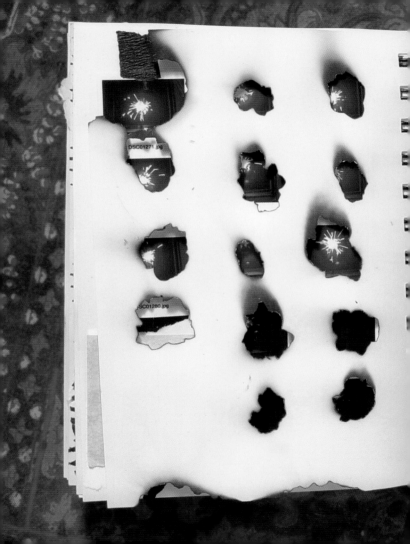

When searching for ideas, a powerful source of creative energy can be accessed by examining the work of others. Look at samples from creative journals, books, magazines and web sites, as well as collections of your own.

However, there are pitfalls. Reviewing the styles and solutions that other artists have discovered before you've had a chance to sketch out a page or two of your own ideas can short-circuit your creative process and narrow the search to directions that have already been explored. On the other hand, ignoring the work of others completely can lead to ideas that are out-of-step or below the bar that has been set by other artists..

Where do you get your inspiration for new ideas? When do you tap into it and how? Is it time to try a new approach?

RELEVANT:

DRAW PEOPLE

If you can draw people,

you can draw.

Why learn to draw people?

Because learning to draw is learning to see, and drawing people requires the keenest eye of all.

DRAW FROM REAL LIFE WHENEVER POSSIBLE. DRAW QUICKLY ON SOME OCCASIONS, SLOWLY AND CAREFULLY ON OTHERS. EXPLORE VARIOUS TOOLS AND STYLES. TAKE A CLASS OR ATTEND UNINSTRUCTED LIFE-DRAWING SESSIONS.

Can't find a model?
Draw a friend while your friend draws you.

RELEVANT:

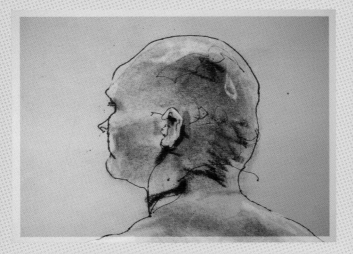

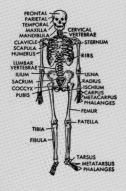

FRONTAL
PARIETAL
TEMPORAL
MAXILLA
MANDIBULA   CERVICAL
         VERTEBRAE
CLAVICLE
SCAPULA   STERNUM
HUMERUS
       RIBS
LUMBAR
VERTEBRAE
ILIUM   ULNA
SACRUM   RADIUS
COCCYX   ISCHIUM
PUBIS   CARPUS
       METACARPUS
       PHALANGES
       FEMUR
       PATELLA
TIBIA
FIBULA
       TARSUS
       METATARSUS
       PHALANGES

Get to know people inside and out through drawing.

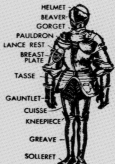

HELMET
BEAVER
GORGET
PAULDRON
LANCE REST
BREAST
PLATE
TASSE
GAUNTLET
CUISSE
KNEEPIECE
GREAVE
SOLLERET

selection

Only one letterform in this sample is complete, and yet the legibility and meaning are not only clear, they are emphasized by the incomplete presentation of the letterforms.

In all art, what we choose to leave out is no less important than what we decide to include.

There is a sliding scale between the subtraction and addition of elements in a composition. Some styles tend more toward the sparse, some toward the stuffed.

With every project, look for the point of balance along this continuum that best suits your message and presentation.

BACKGROUND SOUND

Some people prefer to do their creative work to a soundtrack. If you work alone, or are able to wear headphones in an office or agency, try experimenting with different types of (music) and sound while you work.

Try listening to different styles of (music) for different kinds of work. (Music) that is appropriate during repetitive production tasks might hinder creative thinking at other stages of a project. Listening to a radio talk-show might be possible at some times and too distracting at others.

Musical exploration can lead to artistic growth in other areas. Avoid ruts.

Group environments usually require compromise. If a common vein of (music) can't be agreed upon, you may want to allow a different person to select (music) each day or encourage the use of earphones.

Many artists prefer to do their deepest exploratory thinking against a backdrop of silence. Is there a "quiet area" within the office for this kind of thinking?

RELEVANT:

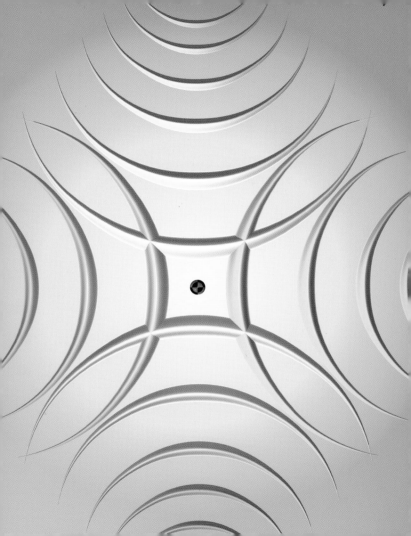

FLOW

"if you
have to
ask what
jazz is,
you'll
never
know."
Louis
Armstrong

RELEVANT:

BACK TO NATURE

ART & REAL LIFE

11

Nature

RELEVANT:

Back to Nature

Slow down; look very closely at the next flower or leaf you come across. Introduce yourself to nature (literally, even). Hug a tree.

Nature is a vast inspirational resource that is all too easily overlooked and/or taken for granted.

Start a garden. Get dirty. Watch stuff grow. Draw, paint and photograph the plants. Smell them, display them, eat them. Gardening engages all of your senses. Expand your sensory palette through nature and watch your creativity grow. If not a garden, then how about a potted plant?

TECH-SAVVY

RELEVANT:

Stereotypically, artists are thought of as right-brained individuals—people who are not inclined toward mathematics or structured logic. However, many of the tools and media of today require a degree of left-brain savvy. Have you explored HTML, Flash and maybe some Java-script coding? If so, how did it go? What about 3D rendering programs, animation or movie making software? If it went okay, then you may be among a finite group of tech-savvy creative professionals who are able to access both sides of their brain effectively: it's the perfect day and age to be YOU.

ART NIGHT

Have an **Art**

Bring out the art supplies and give your friends a call!

This is your chance to make something cheesy and be proud.

Paints, clay, paper maché, stamps, ink, glue, glitter, beads, crayons and more.

RELEVANT:

Night

with friends

Loosen your turtleneck pullover and have an ART NIGHT WITH FRIENDS. If you make art for a living, what better way is there than a no-holds-barred free-for-all with your artistic and non-artistic chums to bring some *spontaneity* back into your *creativity*. Make it a potluck: tell guests to dress for a mess and to bring the art supply and hors d'oeuvres of their choice. *Be sure to remind everyone to leave their judgmental and perfectionist natures at home with a babysitter.* What are you waiting for? Mark your calendar now and send out the invitations.

Here's an idea:

PAINT WITH PEOPLE.

Could this become a regular event?

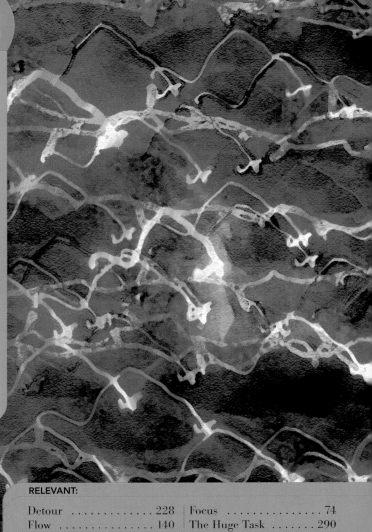

POSSESSED

RELEVANT:

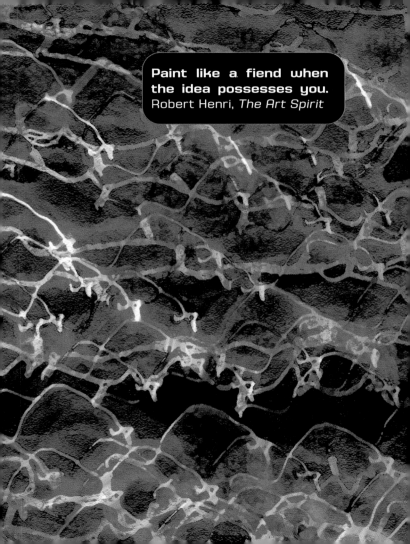

Paint like a fiend when the idea possesses you.
Robert Henri, *The Art Spirit*

All elements of a design or image POINT to something.

Some elements literally POINT. Linework can point to a piece of information or area of interest; the shape of a graphic element can POINT; the visual content of a photo or illustration can POINT.

Other elements POINT conceptually. Certain colors, in certain contexts, POINT to certain meanings. A style of illustration or typography can POINT to particular cultural/societal connotations.

So, if every element POINTS to something, where should you aim them? *Directly through the eye of the viewer and into the soft underbelly of their emotional and logical core.*

Evaluate all aspects of your piece.
Is your aim effective (a), or not (b)?
Is the concept aimed properly?
How about the fonts?
The images?
Layout?
Colors?
Style?
Is everything aimed at the *same* target?

POINT

RELEVANT:

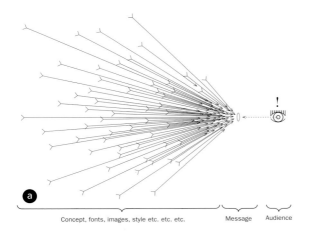

a

Concept, fonts, images, style etc. etc. etc.   Message   Audience

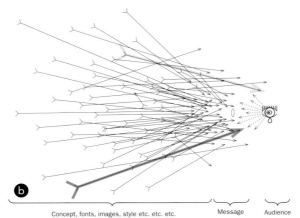

b

Concept, fonts, images, style etc. etc. etc.   Message   Audience

Maybe it would make better sense if you
thought of it

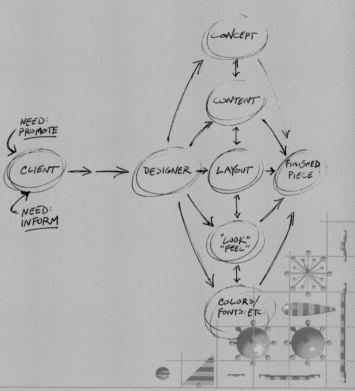

RELEVANT:

like this:

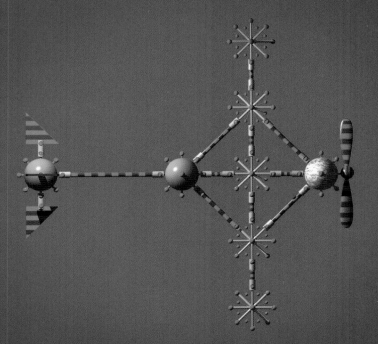

Red speaks many languages, but no

RELEVANT:

other color speaks red.

PLAYTIME

ART & REAL LIFE

12

Play

RELEVANT:

Play with Your Tools

Healthy relationships include time for recreation. Every so often, make time to play with your computer, scanner, digital camera and other fun peripherals. Some of our best learning and creative breakthroughs occur when we play with our tools.

Create works of art that have nothing to do with making money. Lighten up—success and failure are irrelevant during playtime.

It's easy to forget that the tools of our trade, besides being machines for business, also have incredible potential for personal creative expression.

ART & REAL LIFE

TIME OUT

perfect sand, perfect temperature, perfect sunset, perfect water, perfect,
everything. Hey, could i capture this
with just the right combination of
transparent watercolor or acrylic
washes and is that reflection on the
water a true complement of the blue
above and what kind of blue is that or
is it really blue at all where it meets
the sun and would the sun be rendered
by allowing the paper to show through
or would i add a tint how dark should
the foreground be and where is my one-
ita, camera when i need it and, STOP
IT... what has happened to me? if i
don't learn to turn this off from time
to time i will become
something
very
un-useful
to myself.

RELEVANT:

time out.

EROTICA

explore

ERO♂

C'mon,
you know you
want to. Give yourself
permission to create
some art that brings a
little blush to your cheeks.
If you're too embarrassed
to show it to anyone,
don't.

RELEVANT:

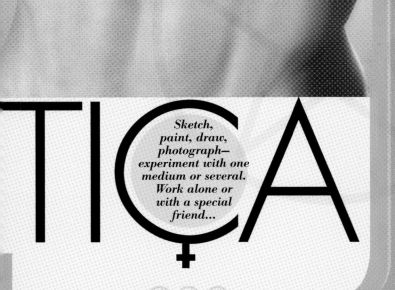

TICA

Sketch, paint, draw, photograph— experiment with one medium or several. Work alone or with a special friend...

GENDER BEND

When we create, we are often unaware that we are working from a gender bias. Men tend to create pieces that look like they were created by men. Women tend to create pieces that look like they were created by women. These are, of course, tendencies and not hard and fast rules. When you work on a project, be aware of any gender bias that might be affecting your output. Be ready and willing to counteract those tendencies if necessary. Bend your gender if the project requires. As you work, consider the audience: what are their gender perceptions? Would they react better to something they consider feminine? Masculine? Neither? Both? Somewhere in between?

POWER UP

Just as a battery's power comes from wires attached to opposite poles, sources of our creative energy are often derived from opposites. An understanding of both extremes gives an artist a deeper understanding of what lies in between.

```
       life < > death
      black < > white
    silence < > conversation
     female < > male
      deity < > atheism
   exertion < > rest
 technology < > primitive tools
  knowledge < > ignorance
    details < > the big picture
        sun < > rain
       pain < > pleasure
    friends < > strangers
   laughter < > tears
  curiosity < > single-mindedness
   concrete < > ethereal
    fiction < > non-fiction
 mainstream < > fringe
     wealth < > poverty
       risk < > safety
     growth < > decay
       lust < > chastity
     future < > past
   darkness < > light
```

EXPERIENCE > OBSERVE > CREATE > BE

RELEVANT:

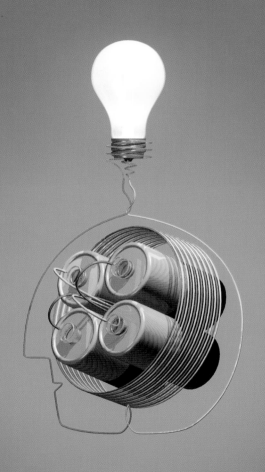

Old-School

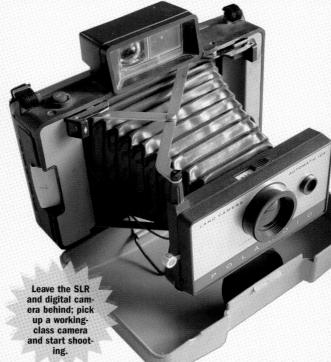

Leave the SLR
and digital cam-
era behind; pick
up a working-
class camera
and start shoot-
ing.

RELEVANT:

Camera ✹✹✹

POLAROID LAND CAMERA

Artists are always finding new ways to use old Polaroid cameras. Though film costs can add up, the cameras themselves are easily and cheaply available at second-hand stores and garage sales. Check out the many on-line sites devoted to these work-horse cameras. Have you heard about the image-transfer tricks that can be done with Polaroid film? Check out www.digitalsucks.com.

HOLGA 120S

A plastic body and lens keep these little gems affordable. These are a cult favorite among those who cherish life's imperfections. Online galleries and local Holga shows abound.

www.holgacentral.com; www.toycamera.com

PINHOLE CAMERA

Pinhole cameras can be made out of everything from a coffee can to a moving van. Go online to find out how and to see some of the amazing things that people have been doing with these low-tech marvels.

www.pinhole.org; www.pinhole.com

PERSONAL STOCK

Build your own *personal* stock image *collection*

A stock image collection of your very own is only a few hundred shutter-clicks away. Get in the habit of carrying a digital camera with you everywhere you go and start noticing and snapping pictures of landscapes, clouds, people, signs, buildings, cars, animals, plants, textures and more. Download the images into an organized system on a hard drive (Apple's iPhoto is perfect for this) and they'll be ready for consideration the next time you need an image or a background for a project. And, you won't have to pay royalties if you use one! **Not a photographer? Look at the work of others...study...practice!**

RELEVANT:

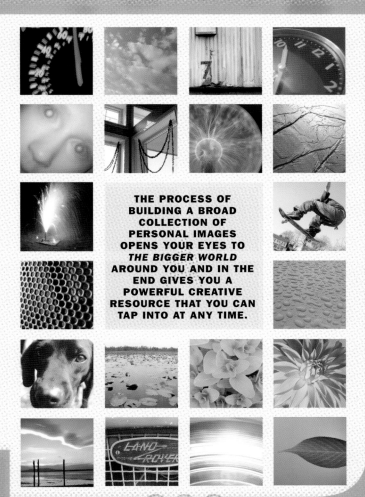

THE PROCESS OF BUILDING A BROAD COLLECTION OF PERSONAL IMAGES OPENS YOUR EYES TO *THE BIGGER WORLD* AROUND YOU AND IN THE END GIVES YOU A POWERFUL CREATIVE RESOURCE THAT YOU CAN TAP INTO AT ANY TIME.

DEADLINES AND RESTRICTION

A cage confining a flower, or a flower making the most of its situation? ▶

Yes, there are deadlines and budget restrictions to obey daily. They are a fact of life for the commercial artist. Our job as designers is to create effective and beautiful communication within parameters set by forces beyond our control.

It's pointless then to dwell on the inherent "unfairness" of deadlines, budgets and other restrictions. Think of them as the boundaries within which you WILL create something of beauty and power.

The next time you catch yourself whining, stop. Instead, try to cultivate the eminently practical skill of making the most of exactly what you are given to work with.

It takes time to perfect this mind-set. Start.

RELEVANT:

There are endless forks in the road along any creative pathway. Investigate as many as you can en route to a final destination. If you use a computer to create images and layouts, you have a degree of exploratory freedom never before enjoyed by artists of "traditional" media. Take advantage! Use layers in

FORK

vector- or pixel-based programs; play with settings, arrangements, colors, size variations, conceptual alternatives and more. If you want to follow a creative hunch into new territory don't hesitate to save a document under a new name and follow your instincts to wherever they may lead. If you don't go, you'll never know.

RELEVANT:

EXPLORE

ART'S REAL LIFE

13

Explore

RELEVANT:

Explore Art

The static routine of the workplace can narrow our minds. Enlarge your creative scope through regular explorations of the vast territory known as The World of Art (both past and present).

Exploring art is a lifetime journey.

When you explore art, travel lightly: leave preconceptions and opinions behind. Explore galleries, museums, bookstores (new and used), libraries, artist's studios. Meet other designers and find out what they are doing now and what has influenced them in the past. Many cities host a gallery walk at least once a month. How about an art history class?

Art & Real Life

FUNCTIONAL FORM

If you haven't begun to do so already, start looking for and noting objects and entities whose form is entirely a result of their function. This is sublime beauty; one that spans culture and time. Tuning in to this aesthetic sharpens your ability to create artwork that is, itself, a pure result of it's function, whether that function is to inform, persuade, please, provoke or entertain.

A pencil

A crayon

A '64 Land Rover

A guitar

A pocket knife

A hammer

A racing bike

An athlete

A bowling ball

A baseball mitt

A pinecone

A saxophone

An elephant

An amoeba

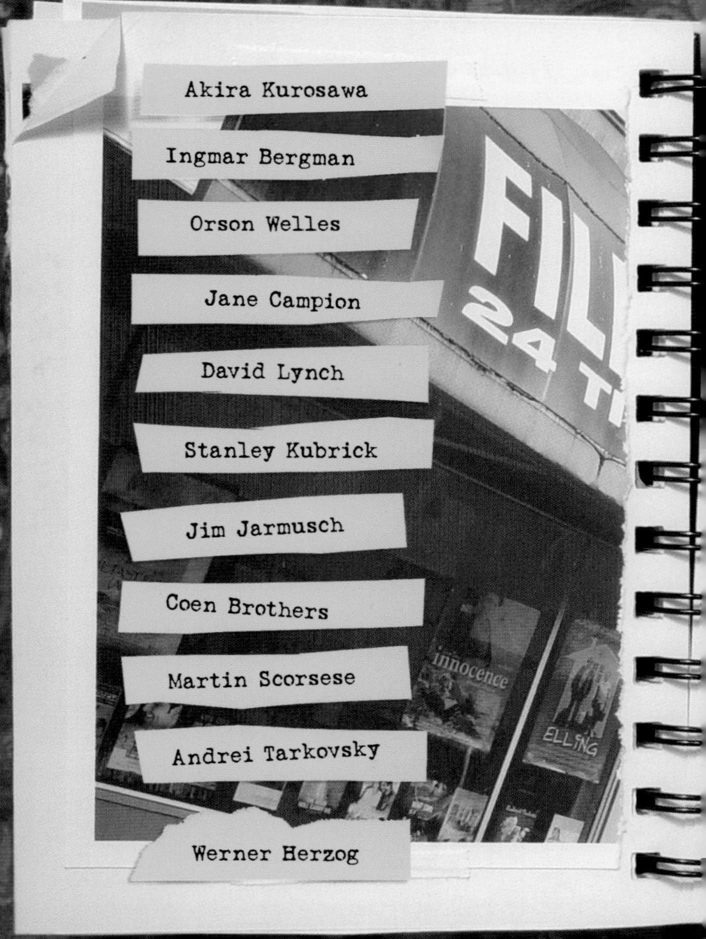

FILM IS TRUTH

Akira Kurosawa

Ingmar Bergman

Orson Welles

Jane Campion

David Lynch

Stanley Kubrick

Jim Jarmusch

Coen Brothers

Martin Scorsese

Andrei Tarkovsky

Werner Herzog

RELEVANT:

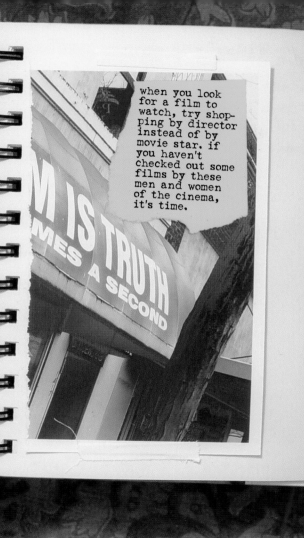

when you look
for a film to
watch, try shop-
ping by director
instead of by
movie star. if
you haven't
checked out some
films by these
men and women
of the cinema,
it's time.

CONCEPTS

TRUTH IN FORM

CONTENT = WHAT YOU ARE SAYING
FORM = HOW YOU ARE SAYING IT

Content is king. Content is the tip of the pyramid. **Form** is the base and structure of the pyramid and must at all times point to and support the tip.

Decide what a piece is going to say and who it is going to say it to. Then search for the best ways to present it through image, color, layout and type. A design element is only "right" if it fully honors the message in look, feel and form.

Judging whether an element is right or not is sometimes based on intuitive criteria; sometimes logic. Effective intuition and logic are the result of observation, practice and study.

RELEVANT:

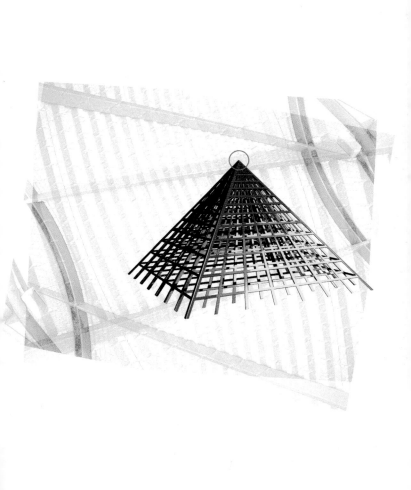

RELATE, REFLECT

every element reflecting the essence of a central theme and every other element...

Cultivate an awareness of the reflections that artists (of all sorts) utilize in their work. Note how these relationships are achieved and the varying degrees to which they can exist within a piece.

ASK: *Does my piece have a theme? In how many ways can, or should, this theme be reflected?*

RELEVANT:

Example:
A fuse can be lit and extinguished only so many times before it reaches the explosive charge.

This theme lies at the heart of *The Wild Bunch,* released in 1969, directed by Sam Peckinpah. From opening credits to final climax, this movie provides an example of the depths and degree of variation to which a theme can be incorporated, both literally and conceptually, into the action of a story and the interactions between its characters.

Check it out.

MAKE FACES

Make

No other subject has received as much attention from artists than the human face. The language of the face is the most cross-cultural of all human languages and its dialects are endless. Don't you think you should spend some time learning "face speak?"

Try this: using the tool of your choice (pen, pencil, mouse, stick), draw 9 faces within roughly the same "style." Work fast, strive for variety within the unity of the style. Next time, try another style or continue in the same vein. Do this anytime you find yourself with a few minutes without something better to do.

Keep your eyes open for both contemporary and historic styles and methods of rendering the face. No other subject matter has been more thoroughly explored. Ideas abound.

Work in ink, pencil, paint and electronic media. Work with paper, pixels, chalk and anything else that can leave a mark. Notice how different media force different solutions. How far would your artistic and communicative abilities progress if you drew a thousand faces during the next year?

RELEVANT:

FACES

YOUR TURN!

In a photograph, lighting makes direct inferences about the subject's larger environment and context. **Is the lighting and setting in your photograph true to the message of your piece? What about the digital treatments used to enhance the image? Do they enforce the message or are they merely gimmicks? An audience is most likely to respond positively to an image that they can relate to—an image that seems to be an honest portrayal of something they can identify with.** A photo that is inappropriately shot or presented gives viewers an impression of contrivance and dis-honesty and is less likely to gain their attention and trust.

HONESTY

RELEVANT:

THE WHY TEST

Effective artists and designers are not afraid to question all of the conceptual and visual decisions they make during the execution of a project.

Sometimes the questions are consciously asked, sometimes not.

"Is green the perfect color here?"
"Is this the perfect green?"
"Is the headline too large?"

Simple questions such as these often lead to exceptional alternatives to solutions that are otherwise merely "good."

Keep in mind, too, that it's okay to hold back the questions until a certain stage of the creative process has been reached so as not to hinder the flow of ideas. But in the end, question everything: concept, content, structure, colors, typography, size relationships, wording, positioning, style...

RELEVANT:

NON CONFORMITY

ART & REAL LIFE

14

NonConformity

RELEVANT:

NonConformity

As artists and designers, we seem to be socially entitled to limit the degree to which we conform to the regulations and expectations of society. Why not take advantage of this entitlement?

How willing ARE you to step outside the "norm" when it comes to your work and your life? Should your limits be stretched? Yes? No?

Granted, as commercial artists, we must often take the opinions of others into account, but do we know how and when to ignore the critics? Question the status quo: follow it when you must, slay it when you can.

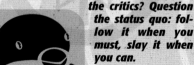

ART 3 REAL LIFE

BAD?CHOICES

RELEVANT:

okay, so you're normally perfect and free of "bad" habits. (right?) well how about allowing a little stroll on the wild side every now and then? smoke that fine nicaraguan cigar. share it with a special friend. share a bottle of red wine while you're at it (rule of thumb: good wine and a good cigar cost about the same.) heck, share a bath with your special friend while you're sharing the smoke and wine. and, how about turning the stereo up to 11 while you're enjoying all of the other fine pleasures? the well-rounded artist has more than a few diverse life-experiences under his or her belt and not all of them would be healthy if prac-ticed regularly. what does your list of forbidden or restricted pleasures include? what are you waiting for...?

ARCHITECTURE

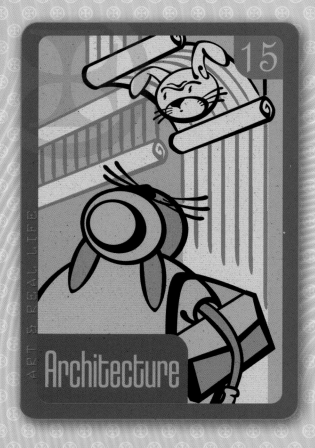

15

ART & REAL LIFE

Architecture

RELEVANT:

Architects are artists, some great, some minor, and their gallery is open at all hours, year-round.

Many of us pass through cities every day without noticing the buildings, bridges and bus stops that are sometimes themselves glorious works of art.

Look at buildings, old and new. Look at the whole of structures and look at their details. Look at the shapes, structures, colors and materials that are used today and compare them to those used in the past. Look at the magazines and literature of architecture. Look!

SOMETHING NEW

Something New

16

An assignment:

Identify a part of your daily routine where you find yourself in the same place, looking at the same "view" day after day. The bus stop, the route to work, your office, a certain window, the lunch counter, the gym, the living room. The next time you are there, look around until you see something that you either haven't noticed before, or that you had forgotten was there. Do this every time you are in that space. Make it a ritual.

The depth of your findings will astonish you. The ability to SEE grows with practice.

ART & REAL LIFE

DESKTOP SCANNING

Create interesting pictures with your

desktop

YOUR DESKTOP SCANNER CAN DO A WHOLE LOT MORE THAN SCAN TEXT AND IMAGES FROM SHEETS OF PAPER.

CHECK THIS OUT:

A scanner, a glass ashtray, and some flowers.

The big flower is placed directly on the scanner's bed.

Here, an onion sitting in puddles of water is scanned at high resolution to create a tasty image. The possibilities are endless. Explore, experiment!

A scanner's depth-of-field is extremely shallow. This means that only things touching or very close to the glass will be in perfect focus. You may want to cover the glass with a very thin sheet of clear mylar to protect it from scratches.

RELEVANT:

scanner

The glass ashtray is placed over the flower. Why not?

A scattering of small flowers...

The lid is closed and the objects are scanned. Fabric or paper can be used in place of the scanner's lid.

A gradient map applied to the previous image yields interesting results.

Hue, Saturation and Level controls were adjusted to achieve this image. *Not bad for a photo taken without a camera.*

Presto. Colors are hard to predict when scanning objects in this manner. That's where Photoshop comes in.

Connect your eyes to your hands through

Contour Drawing

Contour drawing is the name given to the practice of drawing while looking at the subject, not the paper. It is a way of teaching your eye to follow a form and your hand to follow your eye. Sometimes the results don't look like much of anything. Sometimes the results have a beauty quite unique to this style of drawing. Regardless of the results, the point here is to **teach your eye to see and your hand to follow what you are seeing.** It also happens to be a good way to relieve stress. Give it a try and see for yourself.

RELEVANT:

JUXTAPOSE

It is human nature to take note of unnatural associations and to look for the meanings behind their relationships. Juxtaposition is sometimes humorous, sometimes poignant and very often eye-catching. Would certain juxtapositions of words or images add to the message of a piece you are working on? Brainstorm a list of potential visual and conceptual items and look for interesting combinations among them.

RELEVANT:

Notice how the reversal of the juxtaposed elements used in these illustrations leads to two entirely different messages.

TEASE

Sometimes it's okay to tease. Tease by cropping images until they are barely recognizable. Tease through a headline or wordplay that requires a certain degree of thought. **Tease by forcing the viewer to solve a visual riddle.** Tease, but never to the point where a viewer might lose interest and take their attention elsewhere.

STAY PUT

RELEVANT:

whoa. where do you think you're going? sit. stay. work! oh, the things we do to avoid doing things! it's amazing how often the better ideas seem to come just when we think we can't spend a moment longer at the canvas or keyboard.

sit! stay! work!! a favorite moment in the movie "Vincent and Theo"—Tim Roth plays Van Gogh—takes place when

Vincent is part of a life-drawing class and the model has fallen asleep. everyone else has left the studio for a break and Van Gogh, oblivious to the fact that he is the only one still working, pulls his chair and sketch pad closer to the dormant model and continues to sketch her form—drawing, working, searching.

on the other hand... (next page)

GET OUT, NOW!

RELEVANT:

there is a point where the tires are
spinning and the engine is burning
oil and it's time to shut it down or try
something completely different. sometimes you find yourself going down a
certain creative road wondering, "is
this the right road at all? what if i
keep going? is the solution just ahead
or did i miss the turnoff? should i
take the next left?" pull over. get
out, now. take a break. give yourself
permission to

Force Quit...

hang out by the water cooler or the
coffee pot for a few minutes. go have a
snack or lunch. look at a pop-culture
magazine or a national geo. run around
the block. meditate. play the guitar or
bongos. go for a swim. hacky sack with
a co-worker. yodel in the stairwell.
before you actually leave your work-
station though, repeat this mantra
three times to yourself: "there are a
million solutions out there, somewhere.
all i need are one or two and when i
come back to this, i'll find at least
that many.

OVERACHIEVE

Consider:

Finishing the project (early) (seriously).
Then, spend the extra time reviewing,
reworking and making everything better.

+

Striving to create a layout or piece of
artwork so beautiful, so far (above) the
client's expectations that it will blow
their mind.

+

Putting in however many hours it takes
(regardless of net pay) to create a piece
of utter (beauty.)

+

Making (overachievement) your routine. .

RELEVANT:

A layout or piece of art is finished

when nothing can be added to boost
the message and nothing that takes
away from the message remains.

In other words, perfection is
attained when a piece cannot
be enhanced by the addition,
subtraction or modification of
any element.

PERFECTION

Perfect Martini

8-10 parts dry gin
1 part dry vermouth
1 part sweet vermouth
crushed ice
olive or lemon twist
    (for garnish)

Shake or stir gin and
vermouth with ice and
strain into a chilled
martini glass. Garnish
with olive or lemon
twist.

RELEVANT:

Vitality

Vitality

17

Artists, as a group, are not known for being role-models of healthy living. And you probably weren't expecting to find a plug for healthy habits in a book about creativity. But why not?

Are our bodies and minds not the most indispensible creative tools we possess?

Motherly advice: avoid a sugar-coated breakfast if it leads to a mid-morning slump. Seek the perfectly balanced lunch that won't let you down by 3:00. Limit snacks and make them healthy. Exercise for a half hour every day. Consider walking or biking to work. Get enough sleep. Relax!

BEING GOOD

RELEVANT:

another tough life-choice: choose
to be really good at two or three
things or so-so at several things.
being "good" at something is rela-
tive: it's a matter of how we compare to the next person doing
that thing. the winners are usually the ones who spend more time
and energy in pursuit of the
high mark. this means that they
are usually the ones who are not
trying to "win" several events at
once. the most talented among us
are good at one, two or maybe(!)
three things. yes, there are people who are good at everything,
but i'm not one of them. are you?
it's tough to narrow down the
choices: it's a commitment to focus
on the development of one set of
skills at the exclusion of others.
choose carefully and don't go
half way once you do.

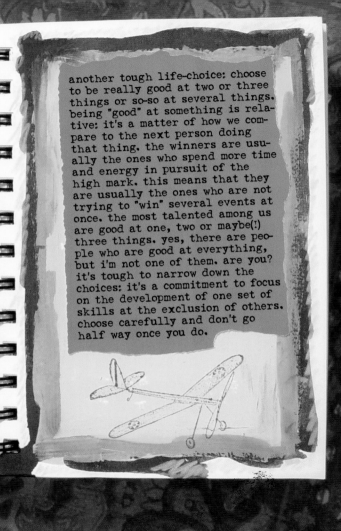

FREELANCE STRESS

10 Top
stress factors of the freelance artist:

1) Not enough work

2) Too much work

3) Accounting

4) Taxes

5) When clients don't pay on time

6) Not being able to pay vendors on time

7) When you can't leave your work behind

8) When you can't get into your work

9) Fear of a creative slump

10) _____

Notes to self: Stress is natural but can be tamed. Develop ways to deal with the business world. Don't go crazy. There is humor in everything. Other careers suck too, but at least (you) get to use crayons.

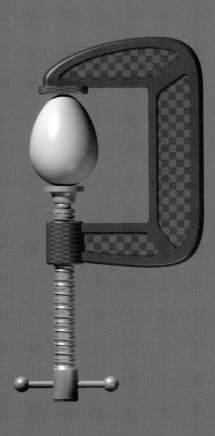

DISAPPEAR

When an actor gives a great performance, you see the character; not the person playing the character.

A designer, too, must realize when it's time to disappear and leave center stage to the message being presented.

Do you sometimes notice pieces that seem to be showcasing the artist or designer's talent, rather than the client's message?

Do you ever look back at a piece of your own and realize that your presentation, though perhaps well done, had more to do with your personal tastes than the tastes of the intended audience?

Don't be afraid to disappear.
Great artists do it all the time.

RELEVANT:

MOTIVATE

if this looks like fun to you, you

RELEVANT:

might have what it takes to
thrive as a freelancer.

BURNOUT

RELEVANT:

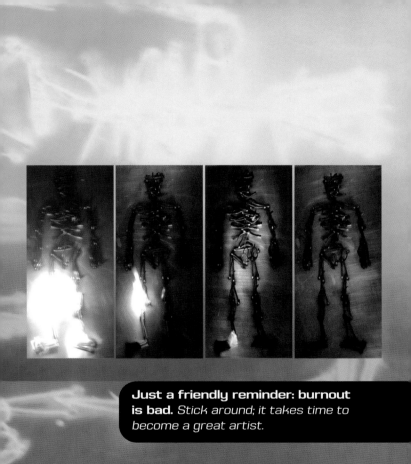

Just a friendly reminder: burnout is bad. *Stick around; it takes time to become a great artist.*

CATALOG

Devise a (system) for saving intriguing thumbnail sketches, unused logos, preliminary doodles, clever headline ideas, word combinations, random creative thoughts and future project ideas.

If the computer is used to store these images and ideas, create an electronic or printed catalog--something that you can look through for (inspiration) or when you need help finding a (quick solution) for an urgent project.

If you prefer paper, create a filing system to organize your growing collection of material. Visit an office store to acquaint yourself with the latest filing fads.

Keep ideas and idea-starters organized and accessible so that the raw-material within is (easily) (and (likely) to be) recovered.

Over time, this collection may become one of your most (valuable) artistic assets.

RELEVANT:

DETOUR

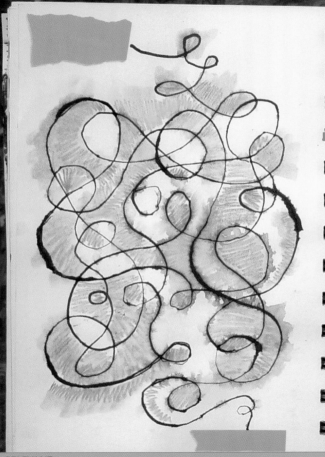

RELEVANT:

it's hard to stay on-task when so many things look like fun—when there are so many areas and projects that seem worth exploring creatively. as a freelancer (free of the watchful eyes of art directors and account managers) how many times do we catch ourselves side-tracked with a doodle, sketch or even a full-blown personal art project in the middle of the work day? oh, the guilt! but wait a minute... MAYBE IT'S OKAY to take a scenic detour along the way every once in a while. how will artistic growth happen if it's squashed every time a new idea begins to germinate? it's a tough call sometimes: work on work, or work on a really hot art project? when we are lucky enough to see the two options merge, we are reminded of why we love this profession.

ORGANIZED CHAOS

RELEVANT:

Organized Chaos 18

Worthwhile ideas, some fully formed, some seedlings of greater thoughts, arrive in our heads at random and unpredictable moments and join the countless others already there. Some are remembered, some are lost in the chaos of the creative head.

Have you ever considered establishing a system of recording inspirational ideas and concepts for future reference?

Consider a notebook or journal. File folders of project ideas, sketches, philosophical musings, quips, grand schemes. A bulletin board of notes and clippings. A chalkboard. A shrine.

SPACE

Don't underestimate the power that white space has for bringing attention to a design element.

And if you prefer black space, don't forget that there is more than one way to convey "black."

KER

BIG

Here's a concept with many potential applications: Take something small and make it big.

For instance, start with a tiny piece of artwork and enlarge it dramatically. The resulting image will have a style and interest all its own. Or, what about identifying an obscure detail of the product you are promoting or the message you are presenting, and promoting it to headline status? Keep your mind open to possibilities like these when you brainstorm your next project.

Think big.

236

PRACTICAL MATTERS

RESTRAINT

RELEVANT:

Attention 302
Filling the Void 40
Space 232
The Unexpected 248

When everyone shouts, no one is heard. When every element in a lay-out cries for attention, nothing stands out. **WITHOUT RESTRAINT,** emphasis is lost.

AUDIO COLLAGE

Audio

Our picture of the world is taken through the "lenses" of each of our senses, and just as drawing and taking photos opens our eyes to our visual surroundings, our audio-awareness can be increased by capturing the sounds of our environment. Keep a small digital or analog recorder (often available on-the-cheap at thrift stores) handy and use it to record the soundtrack of life: music, voices, the radio, your own thoughts, the thoughts of others. Splice into, over and alongside these recorded sounds with layers of new sounds until an entire tape (or media card) is full. In the end, you will have a collage, not of images, but of sounds. If you are multi-media savvy, consider combining this audio collage with motion or still images...

TURN DOWN YOUR "CONTROL FREAK" KNOB:
EMBRACE RANDOMNESS WITH THIS EXERCISE.

OFF

HI

LO

RELEVANT:

Collage

Music, voices, sounds of all kinds—cut, spliced and transformed into a tapestry for the ear to enjoy.

EVERYWHERE

the teacher critiques our work. i
critiqued from my seat as well.

**that one is good. that
artist is better than i am
(for now...). over there,
that layout sucks. that
artist is a
lesser artist.**

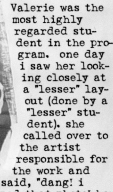

Valerie was the
most highly
regarded stu-
dent in the pro-
gram. one day
i saw her look-
ing closely at
a "lesser" lay-
out (done by a
"lesser" stu-
dent). she
called over to
the artist
responsible for
the work and
said, "dang! i
LOVE how you cropped that photo! how
did you think of that?!" i was
stunned and humbled: my snob-
bery had made me blind. inspiration is everywhere and as
corny as it sounds: in everyone.

SHIFTING GEARS

A supremely important skill for a commercial artist to possess, and one that has little to do with art itself, is the ability to "shift gears" smoothly.

In one day, a designer may have to brainstorm headlines for an ad, sketch logo thumbnails, finalize artwork for one brochure while making revisions to another, coordinate with illustrators, printers and/or photographers, attend meetings, answer the phone and eat.

Many artists struggle with the agency or freelance routine, not for lack of creative skill, but for lack of the ability to smoothly leave one task behind and begin another.

Try putting your brain in "neutral" between tasks. Begin each new item on your day's agenda with a fresh mind so that your creative energies can flow consistently and effectively.

Strategies: Allow yourself a break between projects. Count ten breaths from time to time. Clear your head (if you can. If not: practice). Leave the studio during lunch. Exercise. Take a short walk out the door or down the hall. Drink water. Socialize. Look outside.

RELEVANT:

CONCEPTS

The image below is not Hitler's swastika.

It is an example of a clockwise-turning swastika that has been used for centuries by numerous cultures to represent such things as well-being, good fortune and spiritual resignation.

Nonetheless, how did you react when you saw this simple black and white image (regardless of which

ASSOCIATION

way it is facing)? Do you think it would be safe to use this symbol today, even with good intentions?

Perhaps no other form of art is capable of delivering as much impact, from a source so condensed, as the symbol.

Honor your craft, respect its power.

RELEVANT:

VARIETY WITHIN UNITY

A COLLECTION OF DOODLES, MADE WITH INDIA INK AND A WOODEN STICK. NO TWO FIGURES ARE ALIKE AND YET THERE IS UNITY BETWEEN THEM. TOGETHER, THEY CREATE THE COHESIVE FABRIC OF A LARGER IMAGE. THE THEME HERE IS VARIETY WITHIN UNITY: A THEME THAT CAN BE FOUND IN ALL FORMS OF ART. LISTEN TO A JOHN COLTRANE SAXOPHONE SOLO. LOOK AT A BEAUTIFULLY DESIGNED TYPEFACE, A GREAT WORK OF ARCHITECTURE. CUISINE.

RELEVANT:

THE UNEXPECTED

We travel through our environment, constantly on the alert for relevant and useful information and material. **When our eyes come upon something unexpected or bizarre, it catches our attention... whether the finding is relevant to us personally or not. Would content that will surprise or even shock your viewer be effective for a layout, advertisement or image that you are preparing? What are some of the words, concepts and images that could be used?** Brainstorm for ideas and forms of presentation. Surprise yourself.

RELEVANT:

RESERVOIR

ART & REAL LIFE

10

Reservoir

RELEVANT:

Creative Reservoir

Over time, our heads become a reservoir of concepts, information and images. When we create, most of our ideas are made up of adaptations, variations and combinations taken from this cache.

Therefore, the more we put into this "creative reservoir," the more we have to draw from when it comes time to create.

Our creative reservoir is one of our most important assets and it should be continually stocked, refreshed and maintained through art, music, books, experiences, interaction, observation, learning, curiosity and our own creative pursuits. Fill 'er up.

WORD PLAY

word play

The creative energy of visual artists can stale from working only with pictures and layouts day after day. Try playing with words for a refreshing change of pace.

Buy or create your own set of "freezer magnet" words • Stretch your mind in new creative directions by exploring the written and spoken language • Take what you create and look for ways of joining it with your visual art • Make up your own rules of grammar and style

Record your favorite freezer magnet poems in a custom-made book

HERE'S AN EXERCISE THAT YOU CAN TRY AT HOME. USING A RANDOM PAGE FROM AN OLD BOOK, DICTIONARY, CATALOG OR ADVERTISEMENT, LOOK FOR SENTENCES AND THOUGHTS MADE UP OF A CHAIN OF OTHERWISE DISCONNECTED WORDS. USE WHITE PAINT TO COVER THE REST OF THE PAGE. THE RESULTS CAN BE INTEREST-ING, REVEALING AND (POSSIBLY) SUITABLE FOR FRAMING.

RELEVANT:

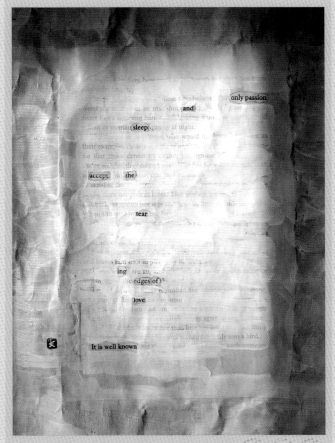

...uose to believe that **only passion**
feed us and calm its mouth-shut **and** ... ... jam
hear like a coursing hare ... ... run
men or woman **sleep** quietly at night.
... ... who would to drown ... ... as
their example slowly so ... ... of guilt ...
the that those driven try create. I an ignoro...
... mentions the correct year. Will this favor ...
accept on the dust too had conclusion ...
what of the ... ... right ...
... they had gotten back? Her woman ...
... but was so her legs and trace or like a phot ...
... is she met and tear ... hair ... ...
... ... tree ... though ...
... ... in the ... ...
... ... woman ... ...
... leaves him and in place ... in ... pass ...
ing are so, ... in...
... ... the **edges of** th...
... ... sounded the ... ... Penelope
... the **love** give man ... ...
... ... and ... ... say again ... ... men...
... ... her than has ... ... finall...
... ... turned fondly **into a bird**.
It is well known that ... ... enchantment...

CONCEPTS

VISUAL ECONOMY

SIMPLICITY IS NOT

ALWAYS

THE ANSWER,

BUT YOU SHOULD

ALWAYS

ASK YOURSELF,

"COULD I SAY THIS

WITH LESS?"

Stuck?

Strategies:

Step away from the sketch pad or computer. Stop thinking about it. Tell yourself, "I will solve this problem. Maybe not right now, but I will solve it."

Take a break. Drink something refreshing.

Look at good design: magazines, books, web sites. Thumb through your files of past ideas.

Turn your back on the monitor, pick up pencil and paper and do some speed sketches. Work too quickly for judgement or logic.

Stand across the room and look at your work from a distance. Contemplate.

Make lists of relevant words and scan for new ideas and combinations of old ones.

Brainstorm with a co-worker.

Go to lunch. Go home. Go to bed.

STUCK?

RELEVANT:

RETREAT

ART & REAL LIFE

20

Retreat

Retreat

20

Many writers and artists believe in the occasional retreat: time spent in a place where distraction is limited or eliminated; where artistic expression and production are allowed to flourish without outside interference.

Could a time of seclusion and focused effort be beneficial to your artistic growth or realignment?

Where could you go? Alone? For how long? What would you bring? What would you leave behind? A sketchpad? A laptop or notebook? Paints and brushes? Books? What is stopping you?

UPSIDE DOWN

lying flat out on the big horizontal rock there's no room for my head so i let it hang back over the edge and find myself at the center of an upside down landscape. the hills and sky are suddenly wide and HUGE and the colors are incredibly intense.

WHAT YOU DO WITH SINCERITY,
PAYS THE GREATEST REWARD.

RELEVANT:

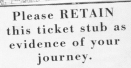

Please RETAIN
this ticket stub as
evidence of your
journey.

1771:3-9

are these really the same hills and
sky that i've been hiking through for
the last two hours? i haven't done the
upside-down thing since i was a kid.
it's good. what other perspectives are
we ignoring?

GET OUT AND PAINT

What are you waiting for? Get out and

LIGHTHOUSE AT FORT WARDEN 6/73

paint

It's not that there's anything wrong with using a computer, but sometimes it's best to shut it down and head outdoors with a set of watercolors to recharge tired creative batteries.

water

paper

food

brushes, palette knife

paints

paint rag

palette

bamboo mat*

Here's a tip that will help you get out-of-doors on a moment's notice: come up with a "to bring" checklist to make efficient packing a snap.

- ❑ brushes, palette knife
- ❑ pencil(s)
- ❑ bamboo mat
- ❑ paints
- ❑ palette
- ❑ water
- ❑ rags, sponge
- ❑ paper, watercolor block
- ❑ water for painting
- ❑ water for drinking
- ❑ sun hat, sunscreen
- ❑ raincoat, extra layers
- ❑ food, snacks
- ❑ (opt.) folding chair, easel
- ❑ daypack

Go far or stay close to home: just get out and paint.

* ROLL BRUSHES IN A BAMBOO MAT FOR PROTECTION DURING TRANSPORT

HOBGOBLINS

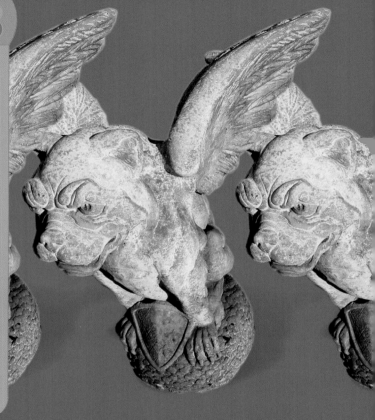

RELEVANT:

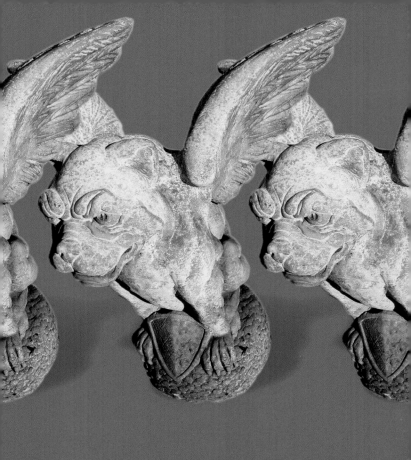

"A foolish consistency is the hobgoblin

STAMP IT

Stamp it

Explore art through household items

This exercise enforces resourcefulness, compositional awareness, color skills and *patience*—useful skills for artists of any stripe. Give the ancient technique of transfer printing a modern twist by using household items to create compositions worthy of display.

AT LEFT: inks, a roller and an assortment of found objects (saw blades, stove elements and a hinge). AT RIGHT: the result.

How about creating an entire series of prints? Second-hand stores and garage sales are a great place to look for useable items.

RELEVANT:

COMPLEMENT, CONTRAST

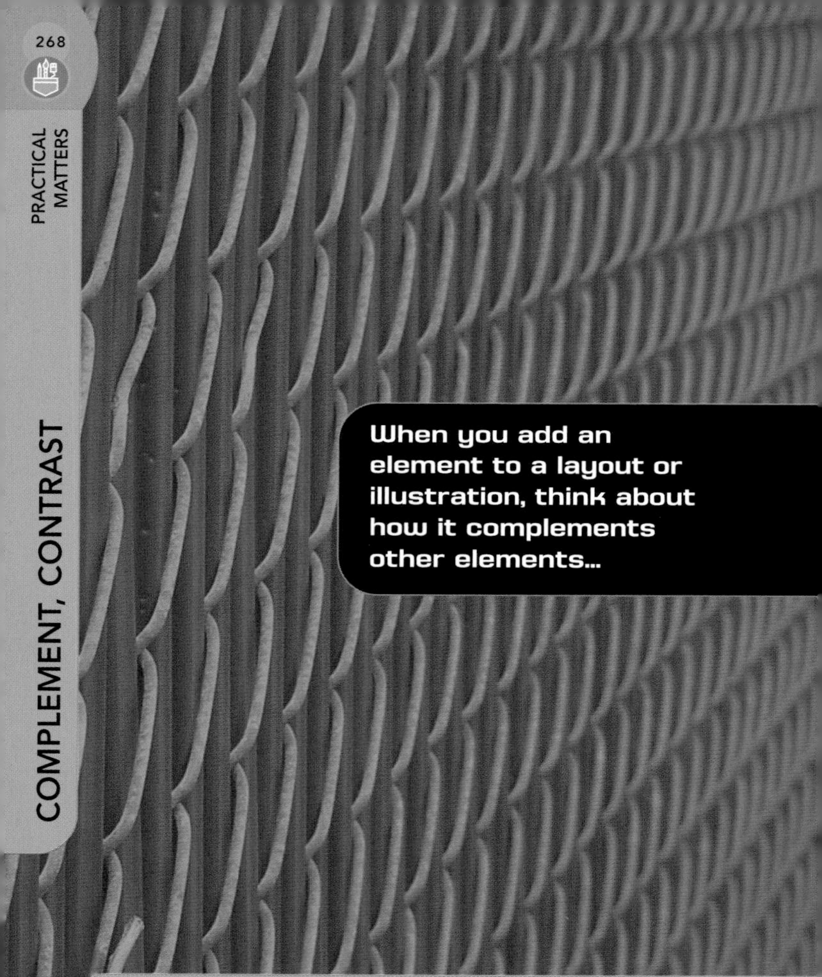

When you add an
element to a layout or
illustration, think about
how it complements
other elements...

or how it contrasts with them. Choose one or the other; don't ride the fence.

VISITATIONS

ART & REAL LIFE

Visitations

21

RELEVANT:

It is very easy to become consumed by the claustrophobia of our daily routine to the point where our artistic growth and abilities are put in jeopardy. One cure for creative staleness is to get out of your studio and visit other artists in theirs.

An immense inspirational boost can be gained by seeing other artists at work and by viewing the results of their efforts.

Ideas: Join a local design or artistic organization and meet other artists. Visit galleries and studios. Attend live music and theater performances. Network.

Art & Real Life

RELEVANT:

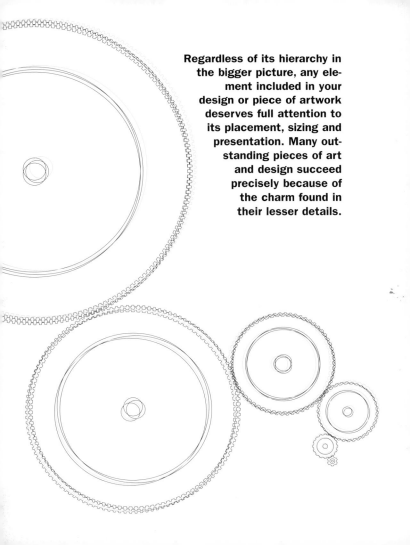

Regardless of its hierarchy in
the bigger picture, any element included in your
design or piece of artwork
deserves full attention to
its placement, sizing and
presentation. Many out-
standing pieces of art
and design succeed
precisely because of
the charm found in
their lesser details.

SNARES

Some snares and blocks to our creative output are obvious. Some are camouflaged and difficult to identify and can sap minutes, hours, days and even years of the potential they hold.

Think about:

The fine line between a coffee break and work avoidance.

The fine line between allowing yourself some slack and slacking.

Overabundant e-mail and phone chat.

Food and drink that give a brief charge and then drain you of energy.

Clutter and disorganization (tolerable for some people, a mental hindrance for others).

Life details gone awry.

What is going on in your life and environment that keep you from your best creative efforts? What can you do to control or eliminate those hindrances?

RELEVANT:

NIGHT SHIFT

RELEVANT:

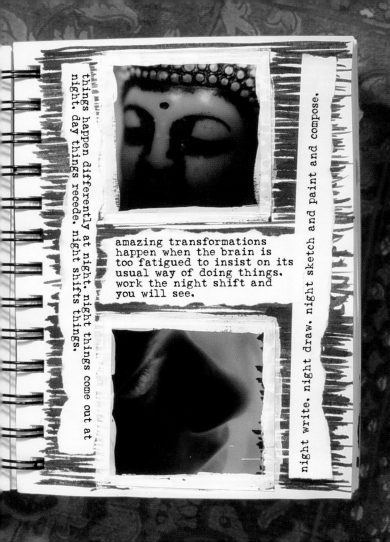

things happen differently at night. night things come out at night. day things recede. night shifts things.

amazing transformations happen when the brain is too fatigued to insist on its usual way of doing things. work the night shift and you will see.

night write. night draw. night sketch and paint and compose.

REALITY

From these three, a client must usually

choose two:

A) speed

B) price

c) quality

You may have to diplomatically explain
this to clients from time to time.
after all,

it's reality

BREATHE

is the wind blowing,

The ability to handle stress is part of the equation that defines the great artist or designer: an art professional who does not find ways of keeping stress under control rarely stays in the field long enough to become great.

Stress will always be a part of the design business. The trick is to find ways of acknowledging stress without letting it get to you. A little adrenaline is okay, but you will work better and live longer if you keep it in check.

Stress reduction is rarely taught in art school. If you need to learn it, it's up to you to find out what works. Ask calm people how they do it.

Take your work seriously, take relaxation seriously, but don't take either too seriously.

Breathe.

RELEVANT:

or are the trees breathing?

explore
Tool
alternatives

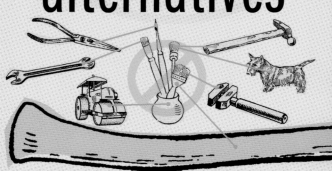

RELEVANT:

Red sable? Soft charcoal? FORGET IT! A pair of pliers or a hammer as a paint brush? WHY NOT? Tools dictate style: push the envelope by exploring tools and objects that were never intended for the gentler arts. Scratch, push, mutilate, pile, smear, smash and crush your way into new artistic territory. Sometimes an odd implement is just the thing needed to give a piece of art the unique presentation you've been looking for.

Before you leave the garage on your way to the art store, be sure to look around for tool-alternatives. It might save you the trip!

Paint with a hammer? WHY NOT?

GOLDEN SECTION

If you are trying to decide how to proportion elements in a design or piece of artwork, the Golden Section provides a good set of guidelines to consider.

The Golden Section is a proportional relationship that exists all around us in nature. Visually, the human body exhibits many "golden" ratios between its parts and features. The natural world often favors these proportions as well in the structure of its plants and the design of its creatures: a nautilus shell, a fern and the human hand are excellent examples. Perhaps it's because we see these relationships so

Want to know more? The web has many sites devoted to spreading the word about the Golden Section.

often we unconsciously learn to correlate these proportions to visual "correctness" and beauty. Great artistic minds, from Da Vinci to the designers of Greek temples and the pyramids, used these visual and numeric relationships to determine compositional and structural arrangements. The following page shows how proportionally Golden measurements can be found.

◄ 2 ►   ◄ 13 ►   ◄ 3 ►   ◄ 8 ►   ◄ 5 ►

RELEVANT:

0 1 1 2 3 5 8 13 21 34 55 89 ...

Starting with 0
and 1, add each two
consecutive numbers
together to get the
next in the series.
This is known as the
Fibonacci Series.
As the series grows,
the ratio between
the numbers ap-
proaches 1.6180...
(the number known
as phi) The Fibon-
acci Series and phi
are the basis for the
proportional relat-
ionship known as the
Golden Section.

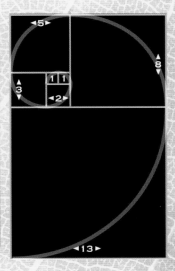

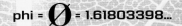

**Dividing a measurement by phi
produces its two "Golden Sections."**

phi = Ø = 1.61803398...

FREE INSPIRATION

ART & REAL LIFE

22

Free

Free Inspiration

Books, magazines, music and art events can be expensive sources of inspiration. Don't forget that there are just as many (and probably more) sources of cheap and free creative fuel.

When was the last time you spent an afternoon in the library looking through books of art and photography? And what about a book or music store that sells used goods?

Consider establishing a co-op "library" with like-minded cohorts by combining your collections of art-related books, music and videos.

WORD LIST

A WORD LIST FOR
BRAINSTORM FUEL.
mix, match,
whatever.
(from the table of
contents of Idea
Index)

action
alteration
backward
bitmap
blueprint
blur
border
brush
cartoon
childlike
collage
compete
condense
conform
contrast
crisscross
crop
crowd
crude
cultural
cut & paste

damage
deform
dither
doodle
drop shadow
embellish
emboss
era
expand
extreme
fade
fill with...
form with...
fragment
frame
gradation
ghost
glow
graffiti
graphic element
halftone
handcrafted
highlight
human
image within
inline
interlace
intricate
label

RELEVANT:

line break	realism
linework	repeat
link	reverse
linocut	scientific
mask	sequential
material	shadow
minimal	shape
mixed fonts	signage
mixed size	silhouette
mixed tone	sketch
mixed weight	speak
mood	spiral
motion	splatter
multimedia	split type
multiple outline	stamp
nature	stencil
negative	symbol
novelty	tessellate
odd	threshold
ornament	tilt
out-of-register	time period
overlap	tonal
paint	translucent
pencil	type element
perspective	type with...
photo effects	typewritten
photorealism	varied baseline
posterize	varied orientation
punctuate	universal symbol
repetition	word puzzle
	words within words

THE HUGE TASK

like an ant moving an enormous
pile of rocks, one load at a
time, i carried all of my belong-
ings to the new apartment using
a backpack. it took two solid
days and about a million trips
up 3 flights of stairs. until it
was finished, i never thought
that it would end or that i
would survive. anyway, it did
end and i lived and it taught
me that we can probably finish
anything if we simply START and
KEEP GOING until it's done. how
are YOU when it comes to the
Huge Task? what have you experi-
enced in "real life" to show you
what you are capable of accom-
plishing? are there giant creative projects that you dream of
undertaking some day? START
and KEEP GOING.

me ↓

the
huge
task.

PHOTO FIELD TRIP

Take a *Photo*

Old-school or New digital?

Go either way or somewhere in between.

Note: A digital camera with an extra media card or two may require extra dollars at first, but the savings in film costs can help soften the financial blow. Plus, "bad" photos can simply be erased instead of processed.

This one is fun alone or with friends. Pack a lunch, grab a camera and go on a Photo Field Trip. Go someplace near or far; inside the city or out in the country; indoors or out. Take pictures and lots of them. Some photos might be useful later for your work, others might end up on the 'fridge or hanging above the fireplace. *Cameras are great tools for teaching us to use our eyes.*

RELEVANT:

Field Trip

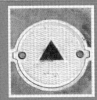

Wherever you go, there's always SOMETHING to take a picture of.

ROUGH IT

Rough

IN SOME CASES, THE BIGGEST DRAWBACK TO USING A COMPUTER TO CREATE ART IS THAT THE RESULTS ARE *TOO* PERFECT.

*****

Look for ways of giving your illustrations a more organic, friendly tone by roughing them up— all without leaving the computer.

*****

FEATURED AT RIGHT ARE FIVE SIMPLE TECHNIQUES. TRY THESE FOR STARTERS AND TAKE OFF FROM THERE.

The original image, clean and crisp: perfect for some uses, TOO perfect for others.

Easy and quick: many vector-based illustration programs (such as Freehand or Illustrator) offer a "roughen" feature to shake up the linework.

RELEVANT:

it.

Sometimes the best way to make something pretty is to rough it up.

Here, a white background has been "scratched away" (see inset) using a "pencil" in Photoshop to give the impression of a hand-rendered illustration.

After applying Photoshop's "ocean ripple" filter to the original image, a layer containing a granular pattern (set in "lighten-only" mode) has been placed above the rippled image.

A messy high-tech look is achieved here by duplicating the base layer, applying Photoshop's "color halftone" filter and blurring the results.

FEARLESS

23

Fearless

RELEVANT:

Much of what we consider art is all about human-to-human connections. As artists, the connections we make have a huge impact on the way we see the world and what we create in response.

Stereotypes cloud discovery. Artists would do well to not only question stereotypes, but to *ignore* them in their daily interactions.

If an artist is to reach segments of society other than "their own" through their work, they need to understand all kinds of people. Continually challenge your assumptions and fears toward others; find points in common; suspend judgement; be nice.

ART IS A GAME

BANK ACCOUNT

Instead of moving directly to "final presentation stage" with your two or three promising thumbnail sketches, consider putting them in an imaginary "safe deposit box" while you continue your search for even greater ideas.

These two or three solid ideas aren't going anywhere: they are safe and secure and they will still be there an hour or a day later. Think of them as your peace of mind--your safety net while you explore uncharted territory that requires more daring than the status quo.

Once you have two or three solid ideas in the "safe deposit box," the pressure is removed: now you can really start cranking out ideas. Look for the obscure angle and explore the improbable in search of the stupendous.

RELEVANT:

LINKS

The saying is true. **A chain is only as strong as its weakest link.** This is particularly true in the world of art and design. **A successful layout is always the sum of many elements that are well chosen and effectively presented (both individually and as part of the whole).** An otherwise excellent layout can be ruined by a single poorly considered element. **Think about it, when was the last time you looked at a design and judged it to be excellent, in spite of lousy typography or a sorry headline?** Scary as it might seem, a single weakness in a design can convey this thought to the critical viewer: **"The good parts must have been a fluke."** Every so often as you work, and especially before you pronounce your layout or artwork finished, stop, step back and judge everything. **Concept:** Is it good—*really* good? **Colors:** Are these the best choices for this audience? Too bright? Too dull? Too many? Too few? **Layout:** Are placements, size relationships, borders and spacing well considered? **Style:** Do the layout and the illustration or photography have the correct appeal and is there harmony between them? **Fonts:** Appropriate? Legible?   ...etc.

ATTENTION

RELEVANT:

Outnumbered but not overpowered. There are more elegant ways to catch notice than through quantity, size or weight.

COUNTER CULTURE

(just a couple of things

to consider)

CONCEPTS

COMMON CAUSE

Every element that you add to a piece has an effect on every other element already in place. As you work, try to see both the **big picture** of the overall design and the details that define its elements.

"How could this new element best be added to the composition? Does this new element's placement leave room for others yet to come? Should this item dominate or support certain others? Should it dominate/support through size, position, color or something else? Does it enforce the meaning and the message of the piece? Do other elements need to be altered, repositioned, added or eliminated?"

Add to the composition only those items which agree with other elements thematically and add to the message and/or informational value. Be prepared and willing to restructure existing elements every time a new one is added. **Experiment, explore, evaluate.**

RELEVANT:

CHECKLIST OF PLACES

ART & REAL LIFE

24

- [ ] botanical garden
- [ ] aquarium or zoo
- [x] art gallery
- [ ] cemetery
- [ ] beach, tide pools
- [x] forest
- [x] desert
- [ ] mountain top
- [ ] city overlook (day/night)
- [ ] nightclub
- [ ] wrecking yard
- [ ] antique shop
- [ ] used book/music store
- [ ] vintage clothing store
- [ ] live theatre, live music

Checklist

RELEVANT:

Checklist of Places

Maintain a continually evolving checklist of places that you would like to visit and experience—places far and near, exotic and ordinary. There are no time-limits or imperatives associated with this list, but it should be honored; try to obey it in time.

The next time you find yourself with an hour or a day (or more) to spend freely, consult your list. Pick a place, pick several. Go.

What about a list of Things to Experience, Art to Create, Books to Read, Changes to Make...? Many people find that written lists relieve their brains of the wearying tasks of cataloging and retrieving data. Write it and forget it.

AIM

Perfection,

or as close to it as we can hope to come as commercial artists, occurs when

we create a piece that makes the client happy, effectively promotes their message

and remains true to our artistic ideals.

Perfection cannot happen every time.

But, every time we design a logo, web site or annual report, create an illustration or take a photograph, we must

aim for it.

Otherwise we are status quo and our creative instincts will die of boredom.

Excite + Experience + Enjoy + Expand

RELEVANT:

Greatness 102
Have Fun 86
Overachieve 210
Perfection 212

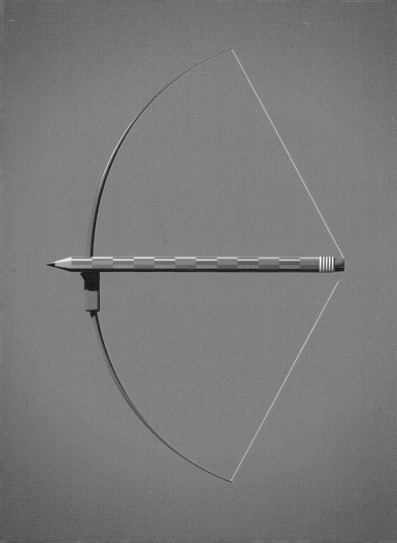

Fill 'er up.